Feel Better.  ive.

STUDENT THRIVE MODE

How to Hack Your Mind & Body
for University Success

PHILIPPA CHARRIER

First published in Great Britain in 2025
by MindHack Publishing

www.mindhackpublishing.com

© Copyright Philippa Charrier 2025

978-1-0684688-0-3

All rights reserved.

The right of Philippa Charrier to be identified as the author of this work has been asserted in accordance with the Copyright, Designs and Patents Act 1988. No part of this publication may be reproduced, distributed, or transmitted in any form or by any means, including photocopying, recording, or other electronic or mechanical methods, without prior written permission from the author, except in the case of brief quotations used in critical reviews or other non-commercial uses permitted by copyright law.

Disclaimer: This book is for informational and educational purposes only. It is not a substitute for professional psychological, medical, or legal advice. The author and publisher assume no responsibility for any actions taken based on the content of this book. Readers are encouraged to seek professional guidance where necessary.

To every student who has ever felt overwhelmed, anxious, or lost, this book is for you.

You are not broken. You are powerful, capable, and wired to thrive.

To India, Hugo & Izzy, thank you for showing me what it truly means to keep learning, growing, and living with purpose. You are my greatest teachers, and my reason why.

And to Tom, thank you for always believing in me and standing beside me every step of the way.

CONTENTS

INTRODUCTION: Activate Your Thrive Mode   7

PILLAR 1: MIND
TRAIN YOUR BRAIN FOR FOCUS & MENTAL RESILIENCE   15

Chapter 1: Understanding Your Mind   17

Chapter 2: The Digital Attention Crisis   35

Chapter 3: Study Smarter, Not Harder   45

PILLAR 2: BREATHE
MASTER YOUR BREATH FOR CALM & FOCUS   61

Chapter 4: The Power of Breath   63

Chapter 5: The Unseen Consequences of Poor Breathing   75

Chapter 6: Breathwork For Success   83

PILLAR 3: MOVE
UNLOCK ENERGY, FOCUS & STRENGTH THROUGH MOVEMENT   97

Chapter 7: Built To Move   99

Chapter 8: The Hidden Cost of Sitting Still   109

Chapter 9: Easy Ways To Stay Active At Uni   115

PILLAR 4: FUEL
NOURISH YOUR BODY & MIND FOR PEAK PERFORMANCE   129

Chapter 10: Understanding Nutrition   131

Chapter 11: The Double-Edged Sword of Convenience   139

Chapter 12: Smart Eating on A Student Budget   151

PILLAR 5: CONNECT
FOSTER MEANINGFUL RELATIONSHIPS FOR WELLBEING   167

Chapter 13: The Role of Social Connections   169

Chapter 14: Social Isolation And Loneliness   181

Chapter 15: Fostering A Sense of Belonging   189

PILLAR 6: SLEEP
RECLAIM DEEP REST AS YOUR SUPERPOWER   205

Chapter 16: Sleep – The Ultimate Academic Advantage   207

Chapter 17: Sleep Challenges At Uni   219

Chapter 18: Developing Healthy Sleep Habits
For Academic Achievement   227

YOUR 14 DAY THRIVE MODE PLAN   243

CONCLUSION: Thriving Beyond University   245

ABOUT THE AUTHOR   249

JOIN THE THRIVE MOVEMENT   250

ENDNOTES   251

INTRODUCTION:
ACTIVATE YOUR THRIVE MODE

It's past midnight. Your laptop screen glares back at you, a half-finished essay blinking. Empty coffee cups and snack wrappers clutter your desk. Your phone buzzes, another distraction. You scroll mindlessly, knowing you should sleep, but you're too wired to switch off. Tomorrow's deadline looms. Sound familiar?

If you're nodding along, you're not alone. This cycle of stress, exhaustion and overwhelm is the norm for far too many students and can leave you drained, distracted and struggling to keep up.

University is supposed to be the best years of your life. But between endless assignments, social pressures and the constant mental load, it often feels more like you are in survival mode. You push through on caffeine and willpower, running on fumes, hoping things will somehow get easier. But what if they don't? What if this isn't just 'part of the uni experience' but a system setting you up to burn out?

You weren't designed to live like this. Your body and brain are wired for focus, energy and resilience – if you know how to activate them.

This book isn't about coping with the pressures of university; it's about hacking your biology to work for you, not against you. Using science-backed insights and real-life tools, you'll learn how to unlock your full potential – without burning out.

You'll discover how to:

- **Train your brain for peak focus.**
- **Fuel your body for sustained energy.**
- **Manage stress like a pro.**
- **Boost your mental clarity and performance.**

Because success isn't about working the hardest, it's about working smarter, performing better and thriving without sacrificing your health and happiness.

WHY THIS MATTERS MORE THAN EVER

Only 4% of university students report having good mental wellbeing.[1] This means that the majority of you are battling mental health challenges that affect your daily life. Nearly half of UK students say university has negatively impacted their mental health.[2] Anxiety, burnout, and overwhelm are at an all-time high.

Western culture is quick to diagnose symptoms and prescribe medication, yet slow to address the root causes of these issues. A 10-minute GP appointment can offer a prescription, but rarely a solution.

Growing research suggests these struggles aren't simply disorders to be managed; they're natural responses to an unnatural environment. Across disciplines, from cutting-edge neuroscience to ancient philosophy, experts are reaching the same conclusion: the key isn't in labels, quick fixes or just 'coping better'. It's about realigning your habits with the way your brain and body are designed to function.

So, what if the problem isn't a chemical imbalance? A 2022 review found no convincing evidence that depression is caused by low serotonin, challenging one of the most widely held beliefs in modern psychiatry[3]. Yet despite this, medication is still offered as a first-line treatment for many students seeking help.

What if the real culprits are sleep deprivation, poor nutrition, chronic stress, social disconnection, and screen overuse? When your body is depleted, your brain struggles to keep up. No pill can replace deep rest, proper nourishment, movement and meaningful human connection.

That's not to say medication has no place, it can be life-changing for those who truly need it. But for many students, the answer isn't in numbing symptoms; it's in rebalancing the system. Your brain isn't broken, it's simply trying to adapt to an environment it wasn't built for.

The good news? You can reset your system by aligning your habits with what your brain and body actually need. Real change starts with reclaiming your wellbeing from the inside out.

THE SIX PILLARS: YOUR THRIVE MODE FORMULA

After years of research, observation and hands-on experience, I've discovered that thriving students don't just rely on intelligence or motivation, they master six essential pillars.

1. MIND
Train Your Brain for Focus & Mental Resilience

2. BREATHE
Master Your Breath for Calm & Focus

3. MOVE
Unlock Energy, Focus & Strength Through Movement

4. FUEL
Nourish Your Body & Mind for Peak Performance

5. CONNECT
Foster Meaningful Relationships for Wellbeing

6. SLEEP
Reclaim Deep Rest as Your Superpower

These six pillars are just as effective and often even more so than medication for reducing stress, anxiety and depression, while also enhancing focus, energy and overall wellbeing. Why? Because they work with your biology, not against it.

For most of human history, survival depended on movement, sunlight, real food, deep sleep and strong social connections. Our ancestors weren't glued to screens under fluorescent lights, surviving on energy drinks and late-night study sessions. They thrived by living in sync with natural rhythms – rhythms that today's world has disrupted. But here's the good news: you can reclaim those rhythms to activate your THRIVE MODE.

EVERYTHING IN THIS BOOK IS FREE

Every single hack, tool and strategy in this book is completely free. You don't need a gym membership, expensive supplements or a fancy productivity app to focus better, sleep deeper or feel more energised. No subscriptions. No gadgets. These are evidence-based, time-tested strategies that work because they align with how your body and brain are designed to function.

Everything you need to thrive is already built into you. You just need to learn how to unlock it.

WHAT YOU'LL FIND INSIDE

Here's a glimpse of what's waiting for you:

- **The truth about digital overload and how to reclaim your focus.**
- **How to manage stress in minutes using breathwork.**
- **Why movement is the ultimate brain booster (no gym membership required).**

- Smart nutrition hacks for peak mental clarity and lasting energy.

- Why real-life connection is a mental health superpower and how to build it at university.

- Proven strategies to optimise your sleep (even during exam season).

WANT TO KNOW HOW YOU'RE REALLY DOING?

Take the Thrive Check-In to get your personal score and see which of your six pillars need the most love.

We'll revisit this later so you can track your progress

WHY I WROTE THIS BOOK

I'm Philippa Charrier, an architectural and urban designer turned wellbeing advocate, mum of three, and co-founder of FAT Properties®.

My passion for student wellbeing comes from both professional experience and personal dedication. For over a decade, I've been creating award-winning environments where students not only survive but thrive.

Together with my husband, I co-authored "Designed for Wellbeing," a bestselling guide for universities and developers committed to creating healthier student spaces. But beyond the design and the data, what drives me most is what I've witnessed behind closed doors. Through my work, and as a mum, I've seen too many students silently battling stress, anxiety, and burnout without the tools or support they need. I've learned how powerfully the right environment and daily habits can transform not just a student's wellbeing, but their confidence, energy, and future. I wrote this book because I believe you deserve better. Not just tips, but real strategies that work.

I'm not here to lecture you, that's your professor's job. I'm here to give you the cheat code for thriving at university without sacrificing your health, energy, or social life. Through research, real stories, and years of working closely with students, I've distilled what works. Think of me as your guide, helping you hack your body, brain, and environment so you can truly thrive, not just survive.

YOUR JOURNEY STARTS NOW

As you read this book, think about one small change you can make in each area. Start with what feels easiest, because small steps lead to big transformations. Your university years are about more than just getting a degree. They're about building the foundation for a life you love.

Welcome to Student THRIVE MODE. You've got this, and I'll be with you every step of the way.

PILLAR 1:

MIND

TRAIN YOUR BRAIN FOR FOCUS

& MENTAL RESILIENCE

CHAPTER 1:

UNDERSTANDING YOUR MIND

'I never lose.
I either win or learn.'

Nelson Mandela

You've revised for weeks. You sit down for your exam. The question in front of you is one you know, but your mind goes completely blank. Your heart races. Your palms sweat. Your brain, which worked fine an hour ago, suddenly refuses to cooperate.

Now, imagine you walk into that same exam, and the answers flow effortlessly. Your focus sharpens, distractions fade, and your brain retrieves exactly what you need. What's the difference? Understanding how your mind works and training it to work for you and not against you.

Your brain isn't just an organ; it's your command centre. It's constantly learning, adapting and evolving. It's not just a storage system for facts and experiences; it's a dynamic processor that filters information, makes decisions, and regulates emotions. Every habit, reaction, and choice you make, shapes its wiring.

Whether it's focus, memory, resilience or emotional balance, you have the power to rewire your mind to work more efficiently. The way you think, the way you manage stress, and the habits you build, all determine how effectively your brain serves you.

This chapter takes you inside your brain's inner workings. By understanding its mechanisms, you'll be equipped to unlock your potential, manage stress effectively, and enhance your wellbeing. This isn't just a scientific deep dive, it's a practical guide to optimising your most powerful tool.

Let's begin by exploring how your brain is working behind the scenes, every second of your life, even when you're unaware of it.

THE BRAIN: YOUR MOST POWERFUL TOOL

Right now, as you read this, your brain is hard at work. It's deciphering the symbols on this page, giving them meaning, and forming sentences in your mind. If you are hearing these words in your mind's voice, that's your auditory cortex working.

Beyond the mechanics of reading, deeper cognitive layers are constantly sewing connections between this information, your past experiences and existing knowledge. While filtering distractions so you can focus, your subconscious remains alert and aware of everything around you, processing sounds and images ten times faster than you can blink. It can pick up subtle movements in your peripheral vision or detect a sudden change in background noise before you're even consciously aware of it.

Without you paying any attention to it whatsoever, your brain controls the bodily functions essential for keeping you alive, like your heartbeat, breathing and digestion. This is controlled by the autonomic nervous system, a branch of the central nervous system (CNS), and it operates every second of your life, whether you're awake or asleep. But that's just the beginning. Let's take a closer look at some of the most extraordinary aspects of your brain.

Memory and Learning

Your brain's ability to store, retrieve and utilise information is fundamental to growth and learning. Every moment, your brain is processing new information, sorting through experiences and deciding what's important to keep and what can be forgotten.

At night, as you sleep, this process continues. Your brain consolidates the day's learning, strengthening connections and discarding unnecessary details. This is why sleep is crucial for memory and learning, it's when your brain organises information. This process allows you to recall events from years ago in an instant.

Incredibly, your brain has the capacity to store information equivalent to 11,000 libraries.[4] It retains sensory details from your past, like the smell of your grandmother's cooking or the sound of a childhood friend's laughter, retrieving them with startling clarity, even if you haven't thought about them in years.

It can learn music and create art, and poetry. It can learn complex motor skills. It can reason with logic, empathise, love or hate, and it can dream and imagine. It can create complex social structures. It can invent physical things and abstract concepts, and importantly, it can believe in them.

It has developed languages and alphabets to communicate with the spoken or written word, and it can both recognise and deliver thousands of almost imperceptible facial or body language cues to add incredible depth, power or subtlety to communication. It can ponder the meaning of its own existence, and it can take you from the depths of sadness to the heights of joy and awe.

Everything from this book that you are holding, to the cities we live in, all began as a thought in someone's mind. Your brain shares this immense creative potential, allowing you to invent, innovate and grow.

Your Brain's Resilience

Each day, your brain generates up to 70,000 thoughts, a constant stream of ideas, decisions and reflections. It's astonishingly resilient, capable of adapting even after injury. Some people live normal lives with only half a brain, while others, after trauma, develop extraordinary abilities – some can recall their entire past (hyperthymesia), while others spontaneously speak a new language they've never studied (xenoglossy).[5] While rare and mysterious, these cases reveal that your brain is built to adapt, grow and rewire itself, no matter the challenge.

NEUROPLASTICITY: YOUR BRAIN'S BUILT-IN ABILITY TO REWIRE

At the core of this adaptability is neuroplasticity, your brain's ability to form new connections, reorganise itself, and recover from setbacks. Even when parts of the brain are damaged, other regions – often in different lobes or hemispheres – can take over, forming new neurological pathways to restore function. This capacity for resilience and growth explains why people are able to overcome both physical and psychological challenges with the right training and mindset.

But neuroplasticity isn't limited to extreme cases. Every time you learn something new, face a challenge or push past a setback, your brain physically changes.

THE BRAIN'S STRUCTURE: NEURONS, SYNAPSES AND SYNAPTIC PRUNING

Your brain is powered by neurons, specialised cells that transmit information. You have around 100 billion neurons, each connected by synapses, tiny gaps where electrical and chemical signals are transmitted.

This network is constantly evolving. Each time you learn something new, your brain strengthens important synaptic connections in a process called synaptic plasticity. But learning isn't just about creating new connections; it's also about refining them.

This is where synaptic pruning comes in. Your brain trims away weaker, underused synapses to make room for stronger, more efficient connections. It's like decluttering your mind, keeping only what serves you and letting go of the rest.

Think of your brain like a tree: each experience grows a branch. Strong, well-used branches grow thicker and healthier, while weaker, underused ones are pruned away to allow the strongest connections to thrive.[6]

Synaptic pruning is most active in childhood and adolescence, but it continues throughout life. When learning a new skill, like playing the guitar or speaking a language, your brain creates a flood of new synapses. With practice, the most important connections strengthen, while unnecessary ones fade away, making your brain more efficient.

This means that no matter your past experiences, your brain can change. Every challenge you overcome strengthens your ability to handle the next one.

Together, neuroplasticity and synaptic pruning work together to allow you to:

- **Adapt to new situations.**
- **Learn new skills faster.**
- **Let go of unnecessary information.**
- **Strengthen the habits and knowledge that serve you.**

Your brain is not a rigid machine; it's a constantly evolving, flexible organ designed for growth. And the best part? You have the power to shape it.

HOW EVOLUTION HAS SHAPED THE WAY YOU LEARN AND HANDLE STRESS

We, and our brains, are the product of evolution. Distinct human functions such as conscious thought, language, social structures, abstract thinking and problem-solving have evolved from the emergence of our earliest ancestors, over 6 million years ago. But many functions, indeed some of the most important for life itself, predate humans. The origins of our brains go back millennia. Back to the earliest life on the planet. You see, you are only here and alive today because the first multicellular life on earth, all the way back to the earliest invertebrates in primeval oceans, developed a very simple, but exceptionally difficult ability: to stay alive until it reproduced. Only those who lived long enough to have children saw their species grow and evolve. To manage this incredible feat, it had to master two fundamental behaviours:

1. The ability to avoid threats and danger.
2. The ability to learn behaviours that help them to survive.

Of course, a multitude of factors influence evolution, but none of that matters much if you die because you couldn't outrun a predator. Likewise, there are a multitude of behaviours influencing evolution: habitat, mating, foraging, hunting, communication and social interaction. But these are all learned. Without a mechanism by which an organism is able to learn, it cannot progress.

Once primitive species were able to avoid imminent danger, and developed the ability to learn. The world was their oyster. They could explore the world and how to make the most of it. New habitats, food sources, and social cooperation gave them an advantage over all the other species.

The better they got at it, the better they did. Those who reacted faster and learned quicker survived. The ones that didn't die. This hasn't faded in time; quite the opposite – it has been honed over millennia.[7] The elegant simplicity of natural selection allows species to evolve to the niche they occupy in the world.

Evolution is, without doubt, one of the most powerful and effective agents of change on planet Earth. It's also one of the slowest. Relative to the timescales we experience as individuals, it's an imperceptibly slow-moving phenomenon, almost impossible to detect. Even the fastest evolutionary changes in humans have taken thousands of years. Most take hundreds of thousands, even millions of years.

THE MISMATCH BETWEEN OUR BRAINS AND THE MODERN WORLD

In contrast, the rate at which humans are changing the world is increasing. From stone tools to fire, metals and machines, each step takes us further, faster. And it's speeding up.

For Homo sapiens, it took about 300,000 years to discover electricity (1750s). By the 1950s, electricity was available across the UK. During the 1980s, computers had not only been invented but become commonplace. Come 1995, we had the internet, and by 2000, mobile phones had gone from unwieldy bricks to something that was actually mobile. Then came Facebook and the advent of social media.

On through the 2020s, AI has not just been developed but democratised to the point that... well, there's no point saying what it can do here. Even by the time you read this, it will be 10 times more powerful.

Today, we live in a world vastly different from that of our ancestors. We consume as much data in a single day as an average person from the 1400s would have absorbed in an entire lifetime. We enjoy more resources, healthcare, education and higher standards of living than at any point in history. We are lucky to live now. For millions of years, it was monumentally harder.

But there's a catch. Being able to change the world around us so fast has created a mismatch. Whilst we live in the 21st century, our brains and bodies are not fully adapted to it. They're a couple of hundred thousand years behind, and some aspects of modern life are not working for our emotional or physical benefit.

STRESS AND THE MODERN MIND: WHY WE GET STRESSED AND WHAT IT DOES TO US

The World Health Organisation has named stress as the health epidemic of the 21st century. Studies show that 80–90% of what GPs see each day is related to stress.[8] But why are we so stressed? To understand why, let's go back in time...

One million years ago, Kaya, a prehistoric human, lived in the heart of a dense forest. She foraged and protected herself and her tribe from predators. One evening, while foraging, there's a rustling in the bushes behind her.

Before she consciously registers the sound, subconscious signals are sent to her amygdala, an almond-shaped cluster of cells deep within the temporal lobes of the brain. The amygdala is crucial for processing emotional responses, particularly fear. It cues responses almost instantaneously, preparing the body to react to potential threats.

The sound is unusual, neither breeze nor nesting birds ruffling their feathers. Using this contextual information, overlaid with memories of seeing predators hunt, Kaya's amygdala decides whether an immediate response is needed. It registers this as a threat and triggers her adrenaline response. A signal is sent to the adrenal glands to release adrenaline and cortisol. This takes milliseconds, whilst the conscious brain is still processing the sound.

Once adrenaline is released, Kaya's body primes itself for immediate action:

1. Her bronchioles dilate to increase airflow and oxygen intake.

2. Her heart rate and blood pressure spike to get her muscles ready for action.

3. She begins to sweat to cool herself down in preparation for the exertion to come.

4. Glycogen is converted into glucose to spike her blood sugar to power either fighting or escaping (or both).

5. Unnecessary bodily functions are not needed for immediate survival, like digestion, are suppressed to divert energy towards muscles and essential organs.

6. Platelets in the blood become stickier, allowing blood to clot faster in case of injury.

7. Blood vessels in the skin and some organs constrict to both reduce blood flow in case of injury and allow extra blood to essential muscles and organs, where blood vessels dilate to prepare for emergency action.

By the time Kaya's conscious brain has processed the sound, her body has gone from relaxed and passive to primed and ready for action.

Along with the physical response, adrenaline creates the optimum mental conditions for dealing with a life-threatening situation. Her senses become hyper-vigilant to detect any further threat. Short-term mental focus is heightened, and decision-making speeds up.

Kaya turns, and her eyes detect a shadow within the foliage. If it's someone from another tribe, she could fight. What if it isn't? Big cats hunt there. As tough as she is, she knows it's a fight she'd lose. Her tribe need her. Heart racing, she runs. Nothing but survival matters.

Fast forward to today…

No more life-or-death hunts. But your brain doesn't know that. Instead of tigers, we face deadlines, exams and social pressures, and our brain reacts the same way.

Take Alex, a final-year student preparing a 20-minute presentation on emerging technologies in business. The moment he begins, he realises he hasn't given himself enough time. There was a party on the weekend, so he's exhausted. Today, everyone in the group chat is still talking about it. He's been tagged in three photos, too.

The group chat is a good distraction from the fact that Alex hates public speaking. In fact, he's terrified of it. Alex's mind is full of doubts and worries. His prefrontal cortex processes the situation and the consequences of not meeting the deadline or delivering a poor presentation. This is conscious thought, but if there is the potential for threat, be it tangible or intangible, it gets sent to the amygdala.

As with Kaya, once the amygdala receives information, it conducts an immediate emotional assessment. It's automatic; independent of any further conscious or rational thought.

For Alex, using contextual information (final year at uni, lots resting on this presentation, the potential impact on his grades) and past experiences (kids laughing during his high school presentation, getting nervous before going on stage to perform, stuttering when asked a question), his amygdala identifies this as a stressful situation.

There are other relevant memories which can be used, ones where he did just fine in a presentation and his teacher was impressed with his findings, but these memories don't have as much impact. The memories of past failures are emotionally painful. It's these that the amygdala uses.

From an evolutionary standpoint, this makes sense. If Kaya's amygdala used memories of a summer breeze rustling the bushes, rather than a sabre-tooth tiger mauling its prey, she might have remained foraging. If so, she would've ended up dead.

Just like Kaya, Alex's stress response is triggered. It happens before his conscious brain, his reasoning and logic, can intervene. It's an emotional response. Adrenaline is released, and the same cascade of stress response reactions is initiated.

But Alex doesn't need to fight or run (though he might feel like doing the latter). High blood pressure and heart rate spikes aren't helpful, and there's no benefit to his digestion being suppressed. He doesn't need to sweat, and his blood platelets don't need to become stickier because his deadline isn't going to result in bodily injury.

The mental response isn't necessarily helpful either. The prefrontal cortex, responsible for logical thought, decision-making and problem-solving, is impaired by adrenaline. A heightened focus on the short-term comes at the expense of long-term strategic thought. Furthermore, creative thinking and emotional intelligence suffer as the brain struggles to understand that this isn't a life-or-death situation. During these moments, decision-making is faster and impulsive. There's a tendency to act quickly without considering the consequences, as the brain is purely focused on taking immediate action.

THE CONSEQUENCES OF CHRONIC STRESS

For our ancestors, these responses were helpful for dealing with the threats they faced. But for Alex, they are not. The 'threat' he faces – his presentation – would be much better dealt with without this stress response.

To cap it all off, for Kaya, the physical exertion of fighting or fleeing would closely follow the adrenaline response, dissipating the physiological changes. With Alex, there is no physical exertion because there's no physical threat. The involuntary physiological responses can't dissipate quickly; rather, they linger.

Our stress response is wired to deal with immediate, life-or-death situations. However, in today's world, these stress responses are triggered by intangible pressures like deadlines, social expectations or financial concerns. These stressors don't require a physical fight-or-flight response, but our bodies haven't yet adapted to the modern environment.

The problem isn't having the same response per se, we still need to have that fight-or-flight response in certain circumstances as we might have to deal with a predator, physical danger and or conflict. These are typically short-lived and sporadic. The problem is that stress triggers come thick and fast in our world compared to our ancestors.

The sheer volume and diversity of potential stressors have increased. They rarely come from an actual threat to life, but they can be continuous, incessant. Work, finances, social media, FOMO, peer pressure, political or global concerns, etc. These trigger a constant, underlying stress without allowing for respite.

YOUR NERVOUS SYSTEM: STRESS VS. CALM

Your sympathetic nervous system is a network of nerves that helps your body activate its fight-or-flight response. It kicks in when you're stressed, in danger or physically active, priming your body for physical action. This system triggers a rapid heart rate, shallow breathing, dilated pupils and slowed digestion, all designed to help you react quickly. However, when stress lingers and these responses don't fully reset, the body begins to suffer.

On the other hand, the parasympathetic nervous system – often called the 'rest and digest' or 'feed and breed' system – works to calm the body, conserve energy and promote recovery. It counteracts stress by slowing the heart rate, deepening breathing, aiding digestion and restoring balance. The problem arises when chronic stress keeps the fight-or-flight system on high alert, without enough time for the body to recover. This can lead to anxiety, burnout and a host of physical symptoms.

WHY CHRONIC STRESS BECOMES ANXIETY

Our brains are wired with a negativity bias, a survival mechanism that helped early humans avoid danger. While once useful, this bias now often overestimates threats, causing excessive worry, even in non-threatening situations. Stress, our natural response to immediate challenges, can spiral into anxiety, a persistent worry about vague or future dangers. Consistent stress results in depression, panic attacks, memory impairment, concentration issues, sleep problems, mood swings, weight loss/gain, menstrual problems, erectile dysfunction, acne and muscle tension/pain. These responses are evidence of a body trying to protect itself, just as our ancestors did. If ignored, they can take a toll on overall wellbeing. So, how does this all tie back to the amygdala, the brain's emotional processing centre? Let's take a deeper look.

UNCOMFORTABLE EMOTIONS ARE WARNING SYSTEMS

Think of the amygdala as a smoke detector, detecting incoming signals and triggering warnings. When alerted, they release powerful hormones, preparing our bodies to respond to potential threats. From the brain's perspective, a panic attack is not only an alarm but a sign that it's doing exactly what it's supposed to do. In much the same way that a smoke detector tells us that our toast is burnt, the amygdala shows us that it's doing its job by alerting us to potential dangers, even if they are not real threats. In a few thousand years, your great, great, great (keep going another 182 times) grandchildren may evolve a strategy for dealing with this.

That's if evolutionary changes match the fastest evolutionary changes that have ever occurred in humankind. Most, however, take hundreds of thousands of years. Many take millions. This is not to be defeatist: humanity hasn't got this far by succumbing to its problems. Quite the opposite. We have got this far because we can overcome difficulties. It means that we can rewire our brain so that, instead of stimuli being micro-stressors, they can be micro-motivators, motivating you to keep going.

Now that we understand what is happening, we can learn our way out of this problem. But learning, the second essential ingredient for life to have evolved at all, is a double-edged sword.

LEARNING: THE ORIGINAL SURVIVAL SKILL

Beyond avoiding being killed, our ancestors developed the ability to continue surviving. This involved learning about surroundings, behaviours which proved beneficial or detrimental, and being physically capable.

We can study this in all living creatures. Insects learn where nectar is based on the colour and pattern of flowers. Wolves learn to hunt in packs. Birds learn migratory routes by following older members of their flock. The ability to learn evolved as life evolved. Or, more accurately, life evolved because it was able to learn.

Learning is, at its most fundamental, the pursuit of novelty. Seeking it drives exploration, which is crucial for learning, as it leads to acquiring new knowledge and skills. Regions of the brain associated with memory and learning are particularly responsive to novelty. This helps you to encode new information, making it easier to learn and remember.[9]

The act of exploring, learning, and discovering skills takes effort, time and energy. It also involves a degree of risk. At best, this is a risk of wasted time and energy, but this could extend to a risk of physical threat, accident, or even death. Sometimes, it's safer not to bother. But life didn't progress by playing it safe. The species that evolved took risks through learning and exploring. They were the ones who acquired new information and skills. They developed a way to reward this behaviour and reinforce it, and they did so by harnessing dopamine.[10]

DOPAMINE: THE BRAIN'S REWARD SYSTEM

Dopamine is a neurotransmitter: a chemical messenger in the brain that transmits signals between nerve cells. It has many functions, but one of its most important is in the brain's reward system. Like adrenaline, dopamine played a key role in early vertebrates venturing beyond familiar territory, driving them to explore, seek new resources and adapt. This same drive for novelty and discovery remains deeply embedded in our biology today.

At the front of your brain, between the left and right cortices, lies a small but powerful area called the nucleus accumbens. Across its surface are proteins known as D1-like receptors. When activated, these receptors release molecules into the nucleus accumbens cells, creating sensations of pleasure and satisfaction. Dopamine is the key that unlocks this system, and novel experiences are a significant trigger for its release. Your brain loves novelty – it's wired to chase the unknown. When you explore something new, dopamine surges, without dopamine, exploration would feel risky, exhausting and unrewarding. With dopamine, discovery feels exciting, even addictive.

It happens in three distinct phases:

1. **Anticipation.** The mere expectation of something new releases dopamine, ensuring that the desire to explore is rewarded, even if we never follow through.

2. **Experience.** Engaging with novelty triggers another dopamine release, making the act of learning itself intrinsically rewarding, regardless of the outcome.

3. **Feedback.** If the experience is positive, even more dopamine is released, reinforcing the behaviour and motivating future exploration.

The genius of the system is that it rewards learning even if the outcome is negative. If failure shuts down dopamine release, we might never take risks or seek out new experiences again. Instead, we are biologically wired to chase novelty, even when it doesn't always go well.

While the decision to return to a specific activity depends on whether the experience was positive or negative, the initial drive to explore and engage with new stimuli is innate. This behaviour is not just a byproduct of evolution; it is a primary driver. The brain's reward system is crucial in reinforcing novelty-seeking behaviours and promoting adaptation, which is critical for survival.

Over millions of years, species inclined to explore their environments – those with the strongest response to dopamine – gained an evolutionary advantage, equipped to find resources, avoid dangers and adapt to changing circumstances. This trait has been refined through natural selection, shaping the survival strategies of countless organisms.

For 99.99% of history, we've never had to contend with the question 'is there such a thing as too much novelty?' because seeking novel experiences took time and physical effort. It just wasn't a thing. **But the digital age has changed that dramatically.**

CHAPTER 2:

THE DIGITAL ATTENTION CRISIS

'I was literally clicking my life away... I was desensitised, enervated, lonely, weary, and way too young to feel all those things at the same time.'

A.N. Turner

It's 2 a.m., and you're lying in bed, your phone illuminating your face in the dark. You've been scrolling for hours – Instagram, TikTok, X. You know you should be sleeping, but you can't stop. One more post, one more video, one more notification... It's never just one.

This is life in the digital age. Always connected, but not always present. Your phone is the first thing you check when you wake and the last thing you see before bed. It follows you everywhere: to the bathroom, during class, while you eat, even when you're with friends. You barely even realise you're reaching for it half the time. It feels like there's this pressure to always stay updated, connected, and in the loop. And it never really ends.

At first glance, it seems like you're being social – chatting with friends, staying on top of trends, and keeping up with news. But your brain wasn't designed for this level of stimulation. Think back to the last time you were hanging out with friends or family. Were you really there, or was part of your mind lingering on your phone? How many times did you check it? Have you ever thought about what these constant connections are doing to your brain and your mental health? In the previous chapter, we discussed how your brain evolved to protect you from immediate dangers like running from predators or responding to physical threats. Now, instead of avoiding lions and tigers, you're dealing with notifications, social comparisons, and the pressure to always be 'on'. The truth is, your brain wasn't built to handle this type of stress.

If you've ever felt drained, distracted or mentally exhausted after being online, you're not alone. Millions of students deal with the weight of being constantly connected. Your brain wasn't designed for this level of stimulation, and the result is something called 'digital overload'. This is a hidden burden that chips away at your mental wellbeing, even if you don't feel it right away.

But here's a question: what if the pull of your phone is holding you back? That digital buzz might be quietly limiting what you're capable of. Think about how much more focused, energised and creative you could be. Better grades, deeper connections, and more time chasing your passions. That small, constant distraction is what we're going to break down in this chapter.

THE REALITIES OF DIGITAL OVERLOAD

Mental health struggles, especially for uni students, are common. Stress, anxiety and feeling overwhelmed can seem like just another part of student life. But they don't have to be.

Recent studies show that a significant proportion of students are now dealing with serious mental health challenges.[11] According to the Royal Society of Public Health, rates of anxiety and depression have risen by 25% in the last decade, with strong links to social media and smartphone use.[12]

On average, students spend around 9–10 hours a day on their phones – texting, scrolling, streaming, and watching TikTok. That's nearly half your waking hours a day staring at a screen.

Studies show that spending more than three hours online daily can double the risk of developing symptoms of anxiety and depression. On average, we check our phones about 221 times a day.[13] **That's every 6 minutes.**

And here's a shocking one: many of us wake in the middle of the night just to check our phones. All these interruptions add up. Your brain never gets a real break. Sleep suffers. Focus suffers. Your ability to regulate emotions suffers. This has a major effect on your overall wellbeing. For many students, this digital overload is turning into a full-blown mental health crisis.[14]

So, why is it so hard to put our phones down? The answer lies in how our brains are wired and how tech companies are exploiting that wiring to keep us hooked.

HOW TECHNOLOGY EXPLOITS YOUR BRAIN'S WIRING

It comes down to dopamine (remember that neurotransmitter that we introduced in the last chapter?). It motivates you to repeat actions that feel good or are important for survival. Every notification – every like, comment, message – gives you a tiny dopamine hit. For a moment, it feels great. But once that rush fades, you're left wanting more. So... You check your phone again, searching for another boost. Before you know it, you're stuck in a cycle. You scroll to feel better, but the more you scroll, the worse you feel. This is called the 'dopamine feedback loop'.[15]

It works in the same way as drug and alcohol addiction – your brain craves dopamine, and when it's so easily accessible, it's hard to resist. Over time, this turns into 'digital addiction', when you constantly reach for your phone, even when it gets in the way of your day-to-day responsibilities and health.

And here's the thing, social media companies know exactly how to exploit this. They hire neuroscientists and psychologists to design features that maximise your screen time. Why? Because the longer you're online, the more ads they can show you and the more money they make.

Your attention is the product. And they're working hard to monetise it. Features inspired by personalised content cultivate a digital environment tailored just for you, entertaining you just enough to keep you coming back.

THE ROLE OF RANDOMISATION

One of the biggest psychological tricks social media platforms use to keep you scrolling is randomisation. Think about scrolling on TikTok or Instagram. One video is hilarious, the next is shocking news, followed by something so random you have no idea how it even made it onto your feed. Unpredictability motivates your brain to continue because you're always chasing that next moment of excitement or surprise.

This technique comes directly from research into the gambling industry.[16] Slot machines work in the same way, you push the button, not knowing if you'll win big or leave empty-handed. That unpredictability triggers a surge of dopamine in your brain. Just like slot machines, social media platforms use this same randomness to keep you scrolling. Studies have shown that when rewards, likes, comments or follows are too predictable, they lose their impact.

By randomising these, the dopamine hits are amplified. It's not about improving the platforms, it's about keeping you scrolling. Apps are designed to build a dependency that's hard to break. Like gambling, deep down you know it's not doing you any good.

DOOMSCROLLING

Let's talk about doomscrolling: endlessly skimming that finger up the screen for content. It's something most of us have done, even though it often leaves us feeling anxious, drained or helpless. Doomscrolling is particularly harmful because it taps directly into your brain's natural negativity bias. When you do this, you also have a tendency to focus on bad news rather than good.

Why does this happen? Because your brain is wired to focus on threats. Think about how you're more likely to glance at a car crash than admire a field of flowers?

Research even shows that babies are more likely to stare at angry faces than happy ones.[17] **Enraging, it seems, is far more engaging.** From an evolutionary perspective, this negativity bias once served a crucial purpose. Whether it was the rustle in the bushes or a sudden change in the weather, our ancestors needed to be hyperalert to survive. Fast-forward to today, and this same instinct can backfire.

In a world saturated by 24-hour news and algorithm-driven socials, your brain is bombarded with threats that aren't immediate or solvable, yet still trigger anxiety and stress. Social media and news outlets exploit this bias. Negative stories prioritise your feed and, before you know it, you're stuck in a cycle of consuming content that makes you feel worse. The term 'doomscrolling' became so popular during the pandemic that it was named the Oxford Dictionary Word of the Year in 2020 (and if you thought that was bad, in 2024 it was 'brain rot', which is used to describe both the cause and effect of the low-quality, low-value content found on social media).[18]

Over time, doomscrolling can trap you in a loop of anxiety. The stream of negative news makes it harder to focus on your day, leaving you feeling drained. As social media algorithms are designed to show you more of what you engage with, the more you click on negative stories, the more you'll see. This reinforces the habit and makes it harder to stop. Doomscrolling isn't just a bad habit; it's a trap designed to keep you anxious and stuck.

THE SOCIAL COMPARISON TRAP

Doomscrolling keeps you hooked through fear, but social media has another sneaky way of pulling you in: comparison. In the past, social comparison actually served a purpose. Our ancestors lived in small, close-knit communities where everyone played a vital role in survival. Whether you were a leader, hunter, or gatherer, comparing yourself to others wasn't about chasing likes or validation; it was about understanding your contribution to the group. The stakes weren't social status; they were survival, gathering food, maintaining relationships and ensuring the community thrived.[19]

Their world was small, and comparisons were with people they genuinely knew, between 30 and 40 people. Fast forward to today, and that instinct to compare is still very much a part of us. But now, instead of comparing yourself to a few people in your community, you're comparing yourself to the polished, filtered highlight reels of millions of people across the world. You're no longer just seeing the lives of your close friends or family, you're bombarded with influencers, celebrities and strangers showcasing their best moments.

Instead of figuring out where you belong, you're stuck comparing yourself to a virtual environment that you can't even physically step into. What used to help you find your place now makes you feel like you're always falling short. The result? You feel inadequate, anxious, and like you'll never meet impossible standards.

THE LONELINESS PARADOX: MORE CONNECTED YET MORE ISOLATED

It's strange, isn't it? Social media was supposed to bring us closer, but it does the opposite. Researchers call this the 'loneliness paradox' because social media gives the impression that you're connected through shallow interactions.[20] Liking a post, leaving a comment, or sending a DM might make it seem like you're engaging with others, but often, it's not the same as having a real, face-to-face conversation.

THE COST OF CONSTANT DISTRACTION

We've all been there. You're studying for an exam, writing an essay, or hanging out with a friend, when – buzz. Your phone lights up, and before you know it, your attention is thrown off. It seems harmless to check, but a quick glance derails your focus. Research shows **it takes an average of 23 minutes to regain your concentration after an interruption.**[21]

All for a moment. Think about how quickly your attention can get hijacked, whether it's by a phone, a tab on your laptop, or even your thoughts. Tiny interruptions add up, making it harder to stay productive. Studies reveal that the average university student can only focus on a single task for 55 seconds before becoming distracted. When working on a computer, it drops to 19 seconds. Simply having your phone visible – on the desk or next to your laptop – reduces your ability to focus and makes it harder for you to get into 'deep work', those times when you are really in the zone. Research shows that even when your phone is just sitting there, visible during a conversation, people smile 30% less, conversations are shorter and less meaningful.

It's not just your relationships suffering, either. Students who used their phones during class or study sessions scored 13% lower on exams compared to those who avoided their phones.[22] The more you bounce between tasks, the harder it is to remember information and focus. One study found that students who left their phones in another room performed better on memory and intelligence tasks than those who had their phones close by, even if they weren't using them.

NOMOPHOBIA: THE FEAR OF BEING WITHOUT YOUR PHONE

Let's be honest, our phones are like security blankets. Whether you're walking to class, sitting in a lecture, or hanging out with friends, your phone is always there within reach. For the majority of students, the thought of being without one, even for a little while, evokes anxiety.

This has a name: **nomophobia.**[23]

How many times do you check your phone, even when there's nothing new? It's not just about staying connected. It's about FOMO. You don't want to miss a thing. Just the thought of leaving your phone at home or running out of battery makes your stomach drop. It's no longer just about convenience; it's psychological dependence. There's a study from the University of Virginia that puts this into perspective. Participants were asked to sit in a room for just 6 to 15 minutes without their phones – no distractions, just their thoughts. Most of them found it so uncomfortable that they said they'd rather give themselves a mild electric shock than sit quietly with nothing to do. That's how attached they were to the constant stimulation.

YOUR BRAIN ISN'T BROKEN

Your ancestors didn't have to deal with non-stop notifications, likes or group chats. They focused on real survival: finding food, staying safe and protecting their tribe.[24] The truth is, your brain hasn't changed, but the world around you has.

While you can't escape the impact of technology, you can control how you interact with it. The first step is recognising how digital overload affects your wellbeing. The second step? Taking back control and unlocking a version of yourself that's calmer, sharper, and more alive.

In the next chapter, we'll dive into practical strategies for managing your relationship with technology and stress. You'll learn how to set boundaries with your phone, practise mindfulness, and find a healthier balance between the digital world and real life.

CHAPTER 3:

STUDY SMARTER, NOT HARDER

> '*Things get bad for all of us, almost continually, and what we do under the constant stress reveals who/what we are.*'
>
> *Charles Bukowski*

Your brain was designed for survival. But while your ancestors ran from predators, your 'threats' today look different – deadlines, group chats, back-to-back lectures and a never-ending stream of notifications.

The problem? Your brain doesn't know the difference. It still activates 'fight or flight' over an overdue essay, flooding your system with stress hormones, spiking your heart rate and clouding your thinking.

That's where this chapter comes in. Instead of fighting against your brain, you'll learn how to work with it – so you can study smarter, stress less and perform at your peak.

Hack #1:
MOVE TO BOOST BRAIN POWER

We've explored neuroplasticity, the brain's ability to change and grow. One of the fastest ways to activate your brain's learning potential is through movement.

Do you want to retain information faster and recall details effortlessly? Move.

Why It Works

Every time you walk, stretch, or even fidget, your brain releases brain-derived neurotrophic factor (BDNF), a protein that strengthens neural connections and enhances memory retention. Think of BDNF as 'fertiliser for your brain', it helps new brain cells grow and improves cognitive function.[25]

How To Do It

A simple 10-minute walk after studying can boost memory retention by 20%[26]. That's why some of the world's smartest people, including Steve Jobs and Mark Zuckerberg preferred walking meetings over sitting ones.

QUICK WIN

After each study session, take a 10-minute walk to lock in what you've learned.

Next Steps Build regular exercise into your weekly routine. Walk while listening to a podcast, stretch during breaks, or use active recall while exercising.

For more movement hacks, go to Pillar 3 – MOVE

Research Insight Students who engage in regular exercise such as running, cycling, or other forms of aerobic exercise consistently outperform their less-active peers academically.[27]

Hack #2:
FIND THE CALM – CONTROL YOUR STRESS RESPONSE

Why It Works

We've discussed how the amygdala, the brain's 'alarm system', triggers stress before your logical brain has time to react. We've also explored how, if it is left unchecked, it can hijack focus and decision-making.

The solution? Mindfulness training. Practising mindfulness helps calm your nervous system, improve concentration and regulate emotions.

The 5-4-3-2-1 Grounding Technique

How To Do It

1. Look around and name **five** things you can see.
2. Identify **four** things you can physically touch.
3. Listen for **three** different sounds.
4. Notice **two** distinct smells.
5. Focus on **one** thing you can taste.

QUICK WIN

Next time you're feeling overwhelmed, take 60 seconds to do this exercise; it immediately grounds your mind. It's a fast, easy way to get your focus back on track, whether you're studying, writing an essay or sitting in an exam.

Next Steps Spend 5 minutes daily on mindfulness techniques like deep breathing or guided meditation to train your focus.

For more breathing hacks, go to **Pillar 2 – Breathe**

Research Insight: Practising mindfulness has been shown to lower stress, improve mood, and enhance emotional regulation.[28] Research from King's College London also found that mindfulness training enhances memory and attention, enabling students to stay focused and retain information more effectively.[29]

Hack #3:

REFRAME STRESS – MAKE IT WORK FOR YOU

We've explored why stress exists – it's an evolutionary survival response. But while stress helped our ancestors outrun danger, modern stressors are constant and overwhelming. Stress isn't always bad. In fact, it's designed to enhance performance – your brain releases adrenaline and cortisol to sharpen focus. The key? Reframe stress as your secret weapon.

- If you see stress as harmful, your body tightens up and your mind panics.
- If you see stress as fuel, your body channels it into focus and energy.

QUICK WIN

Next time you feel stress creeping in, try this three-step stress reframe:

Step 1: Label it differently. Instead of saying 'I'm stressed,' say 'I'm in THRIVE MODE.'

Step 2: Change your posture. Stand tall, shoulders back, your brain associates good posture with confidence.

Step 3: Focus on performance. Ask yourself: 'How can I use this energy to improve my focus?'

Next Steps After each stressful situation, write down what happened and reframe your perspective–this trains your brain to see stress as an advantage.

- What did I learn from this?
- How did stress actually help me?

- How can I use this response to my advantage next time?

Over time, this rewires your brain to see stress as an ally, not an enemy.

Research Insight: Students who view stress as a tool for performance, rather than a threat, show lower cortisol levels and perform better academically.[30] Why? Because your perception of stress changes how your body responds to it.

Hack #4:
DIGITAL DETOX – RECLAIM YOUR FOCUS

Why it Works

We've discussed how your brain craves novelty, every notification hijacks your dopamine system, making it harder to focus. Social media apps are engineered to keep you hooked. Just like a slot machine, hoping for a hit. Each notification keeps you hooked.

How To Do It

It's time to take back control:

1. **Start small**: Try 1 hour of screen-free time before bed.
2. **Expand gradually**: Use an app blocker (Forest, Cold Turkey) during study sessions.
3. **Set boundaries**: Unsubscribe from unnecessary notifications.

QUICK WIN

Move your phone to another room while studying, this alone improves focus.

Next Steps Implement weekly screen-free mornings or social media detoxes to reset your dopamine balance.

Research Insight Students who commit to daily digital detoxes report lower stress levels and better sleep.[31]

> ### CREATING DISTANCE FROM YOUR PHONE
>
> Your phone should be a tool adding value to your life, not dominating it. Ask yourself three questions before picking it up:
>
> 1. Is this urgent or just a habit?
> 2. What am I here to do?
> 3. Will this add value or just waste my time?

Hack #5:
SLEEP – THE ULTIMATE COGNITIVE ENHANCER

Why it Works

Your brain organises and stores information while you sleep. Without enough rest, your cognitive function, focus and emotional resilience take a hit.

QUICK WIN

Avoid caffeine after midday and turn off screens 1 hour before bed.

Next Steps Stick to a consistent sleep schedule – yes, even on weekends.

Research Insight Sleep plays a vital role in strengthening neural connections involved in learning and memory. Students who prioritise consistent, high-quality sleep demonstrate faster information recall and greater cognitive flexibility when facing academic challenges, compared to those with irregular or disrupted sleep patterns[32].

For more sleep hacks, go to **Pillar 6 – Sleep**

Hack #6:
THE POMODORO TECHNIQUE – WORK SMARTER, NOT HARDER

Why It Works

Procrastination and distractions are two of the biggest obstacles to effective studying. Your brain is not designed to focus for hours. After 25–40 minutes, cognitive fatigue sets in and your prefrontal cortex (your decision-making and focus centre) slows down, and distractions creep in. Enter the Pomodoro Technique: Work in 25-minute sprints, then take a 5-minute reset. These mini breaks prevent burnout, refresh focus and improve memory retention.

How To Do It

1. **Set a 25-minute timer,** focus on one task.
2. **Take a 5-minute break,** stand up, stretch or grab a drink.
3. **Repeat 4 times,** then take a longer 20–30-minute break.

QUICK WIN

Try one Pomodoro session today, set a timer for 25 minutes and dive in.

Next Steps Experiment with different work/break ratios (e.g. 40 minutes study/10 minutes rest).

Combine this method with other focus-enhancing techniques like movement breaks and digital detoxing for maximum impact.

Research Insight It takes an average of 23 minutes to refocus after an interruption.[33] By structuring study sessions into short, focused sprints, the Pomodoro Technique maximises efficiency and reduces cognitive overload. Each distraction costs you nearly half an hour of lost productivity.

Hack #7:
SELF-COMPASSION – WORK WITH YOUR BRAIN, NOT AGAINST IT

When university gets tough, it's easy to be hard on yourself. Your inner critic can be brutal:

'I should have done better.' 'I'm not smart enough.' 'I always mess up.'

The truth is, if self-judgment worked, you'd be perfect by now.

Try this instead: Talk to yourself like you'd speak to a friend. Swap 'I failed' for 'I'm learning.' Remember: One setback doesn't define your ability.

QUICK WIN

The next time you find yourself being overly critical, pause, acknowledge your feelings, and remind yourself it's okay to make mistakes. Would you treat a loved one how you treat yourself?

Next Steps Make self-compassion a habit, especially when things get tough during exams or when approaching deadlines.

Research Insight Multiple studies show that students who practise self-compassion experience less anxiety and depression, especially during high-stress periods like exam time.[34]

Hack #8:
GRATITUDE – REWIRE YOUR BRAIN FOR POSITIVITY

Your brain is wired for survival, which means it's naturally drawn to negative experiences and threats. This negativity bias can heighten stress and anxiety, but gratitude is a powerful tool to counteract it. Practising gratitude daily shifts your brain away from fear and stress and into a state of emotional balance and wellbeing.

Why It Works

Gratitude is the antidote to fear, it activates brain regions associated with positive emotions and reduces the grip of the stress response. Gratitude encourages an oxytocin state, it promotes feelings of connection and security, increasing the production of oxytocin (the bonding hormone), which helps calm the nervous system and foster emotional resilience.

Gratitude enhances focus and mental clarity, a grateful mindset reframes challenges and helps you approach academic and personal pressures with greater optimism and problem-solving ability.

How To Do It

1. Each day, write down three things you're grateful for.
   - They can be simple: It's a sunny day, I've had a good conversation, I've finished an assignment on time.

2. Use gratitude to reframe challenges.

- Instead of 'I'm overwhelmed by my workload,' try: 'I'm grateful to have the opportunity to learn and improve.'

3. Express gratitude to others.

- A quick text to a friend, a thank-you note, or simply acknowledging someone's kindness can boost oxytocin and social connection.

QUICK WIN

Write down three things you're grateful for right now:

1.

2.

3.

Next Steps

- Keep a gratitude journal and write in it each night before bed.

- When stressed, pause and list one thing you appreciate about the moment.

- Start a gratitude habit in group chats – sharing one good thing daily with friends.

Research Insight Practising gratitude can reduce stress, improve emotional wellbeing and even reshape brain activity. Individuals who write gratitude letters show greater neural sensitivity in the medial prefrontal cortex, the brain region associated with learning, decision-making and emotional regulation. Other research suggests that gratitude is linked to lower cortisol levels and higher engagement in academic and social settings.[35]

Hack #9:

VISUALISATION – TRAIN YOUR BRAIN FOR SUCCESS

Your brain can't tell the difference between real and imagined experiences. Visualisation is a powerful mental trick. Picture yourself succeeding at something. Can you feel it? The spark of hope? By imagining a positive outcome, you're preparing your brain to handle the real thing, all the while reducing anxiety. Top athletes and performers use this technique to prepare for big moments.

Why it Works

This technique is not just about positive thinking – it activates the same neural pathways as physically doing the task. Olympic athletes have long used mental rehearsal as a core part of their training. Michael Phelps, the most decorated Olympian in history, visualised his races down to every stroke and turn, helping him maintain composure even in unexpected situations.

Beyond sports, business leaders and creatives also use visualisation. Oprah Winfrey attributes much of her success to the power of mental imagery, stating that she visualised her achievements before they became reality. Jim Carrey famously wrote himself a $10 million cheque for 'acting services rendered' long before he landed major film roles, keeping it in his wallet as a reminder of what was to come.

Neuroscience also shows that by mentally 'visiting' your successful future self, you create a powerful connection between thought and reality, helping you build confidence and reduce fear.

QUICK WIN

Before your next exam, take 5 minutes to visualise yourself nailing it. Feel the confidence, clarity and control as if you're already there.

Next Steps Make visualisation a daily habit. Each morning, take a moment to 'visit' your future self succeeding in the day's tasks. Whether it's a workout, a presentation or a challenge ahead, see yourself excelling and stepping into the best version of yourself. Success is rehearsed first in your mind, and then in reality.

Research Insight Students who visualised successfully completing exam tasks had higher test scores and significantly reduced test anxiety, compared to those who did not use visual imagery.[36]

Hack #10:
MENTAL MINIMALISM – DECLUTTER YOUR MIND

Your brain is like a phone running too many apps at once. Every lecture, assignment, group chat and notification is an open app draining your mental battery. If you want to boost focus and clarity, you need to block out the background noise.

Three Simple Steps to Clear Your Mental Clutter

Step 1: Brain dump Spend 1-3 minutes writing down everything that's on your mind. This simple act helps declutter your thoughts and create mental space.

Step 2: Prioritise Ask yourself, "What actually needs my attention today?" Circle the top 3 and let go of the rest.

Step 3: Mute distractions Turn off notifications. Delete non-essential apps. Leave distracting group chats. Create space for focus.

Step 4: Journal Even 5 minutes a day helps you process thoughts, build clarity, and boost your mental resilience.

STUDENT THRIVE MODE

QUICK WIN

Right now, take 60 seconds to list everything on your mind. Then close the mental tabs you don't need.

_____

_____

_____

_____

_____

_____

_____

_____

_____

Next Steps

1. Start a daily brain dump or journaling habit.
2. Use one app to organise your week. Delete or mute the rest.
3. Ask yourself each day: "What's essential?"

Research Insight

Simple techniques like expressive writing and structured brain dumps significantly reduce cognitive load and improve students' ability to retain complex information. Regular journaling has also been linked to lower stress levels, enhanced memory, and greater emotional resilience, all essential tools for thriving in high-pressure academic environments[37].

MASTER YOUR MIND

Your brain is like a dirt track; every thought and habit you repeat carves a stronger trail. These hacks are your tools to pave the way to sharper focus, greater resilience and lasting success.

At first, these strategies might feel unfamiliar, but with practice, they become second nature. Every time you apply one of these hacks, you're rewiring your brain, making it stronger and more adaptable under pressure.

Which of these hacks will you start with today?

_____

_____

_____

_____

PILLAR 2:

BREATHE

MASTER YOUR BREATH

FOR CALM & FOCUS

CHAPTER 4:

THE POWER OF BREATH

'Breath is the bridge which connects life to consciousness, which unites your body to your thoughts.'

Thich Nhat Hanh

Right now, you're breathing. In. Out. Without thinking, without effort. The pace of your breath matches your heart, your thoughts and your emotions. But when was the last time you stopped to actually notice it? Pause.

Take a slow, deep breath. Inhale through your nose. Hold it. Now exhale slowly. How does your body feel? Did your shoulders loosen? Did your jaw unclench? Did your mind clear, even if just a little? That single breath just changed your physiology.

Your breath is your most powerful tool, yet it's the one we overlook the most. When harnessed, it can sharpen focus, regulate stress and boost performance. Elite athletes, world-class singers, special forces soldiers and master yogis all rely on breath control to stay calm under pressure. What do they know that you don't? This chapter will show you.

THE SCIENCE OF BREATHING: A FORGOTTEN SUPERPOWER

Each breath you take influences your focus, energy and emotions. Fast, shallow breaths signal stress. Deep, controlled breathing signals calm. Think of your breath as the remote control for your nervous system – yet most people never learn how to use it.[38]

Breathwork is rooted in ancient wisdom from across the world. Bygone civilisations recognised its powerful effects on mental and physical wellbeing.

We all know that breathing is essential. Shallow, fast breaths prepare muscles for action, while deep, slow breaths allow for relaxation and recovery. This dynamic is something humans evolved to depend on; a mechanism to support our anatomy.

Ancient yogis practised pranayama (breath control) to master the mind.[39] Zen monks used controlled breathing for enlightenment. Indigenous cultures synchronised breath with nature's rhythms. Eastern practices like qigong and tai chi used breath to cultivate life energy (qi).

Science is only now catching up, but research shows that breathwork enhances cognitive function, emotional regulation and resilience. Navy Seals, trained to handle intense, life-threatening covert missions and high-stakes rescues, stay sharp and calm under pressure using breath control. If elite athletes and special forces rely on breath control in extreme situations, imagine how powerful it can be when you're facing an exam, a nerve-wracking presentation or deadline-induced panic.

HOW BREATHING SHAPES YOUR MIND AND BODY

To understand how breathing impacts your mind and body, let's follow a single inhale.

Step 1: The Journey of a Breath

Air begins its journey through your nose or mouth. If you breathe through your nose, tiny cilia (hair-like structures) and mucus work together to filter dust, allergens and foreign particles, warming and humidifying the air before it enters your lungs.

From there, air travels down the trachea (windpipe), a tube reinforced with C-shaped cartilage rings that keep it open. The trachea then splits into two main bronchi, each leading to a lung. These bronchi further divide into smaller branches called bronchioles, which continue to narrow until they reach tiny, balloon-like sacs called alveoli.

This is where the magic happens. Each lung contains around 300 million alveoli, creating a vast surface area – roughly the size of a tennis court – for gas exchange. Oxygen from the air passes through the thin alveolar walls into the bloodstream, while carbon dioxide, a waste product, moves from the blood into the alveoli to be exhaled.

Step 2: Oxygen Delivery – Powering Every Cell

Once oxygen binds to haemoglobin in your blood, it travels throughout your body. Inside each cell, a tiny powerhouse called the mitochondrion uses oxygen to produce adenosine triphosphate (ATP), the energy molecule powering everything from muscle contractions to brain activity. Without proper oxygen flow, focus, learning and memory suffer.

BREATHING FOR STRESS REGULATION AND COGNITIVE ENHANCEMENT

Beyond fuelling cells, breathing plays a pivotal role in influencing the nervous system, impacting your mood, stress levels and even how our body functions at a cellular level. Central to this is the autonomic nervous system (ANS), which controls involuntary actions like heart rate, digestion and, yes, breathing itself.

THE TWO AUTONOMIC NERVOUS SYSTEM MODES:

The Sympathetic Nervous System (SNS) – The 'Fight-or-Flight' Mode

When you're stressed or anxious, the SNS kicks in:

- Heart rate increases
- Breathing becomes shallow
- Digestion slows down (because survival > food)

The Parasympathetic Nervous System (PNS) – The 'Rest-and-Digest' Mode

When you are calm and relaxed, the PNS activates:

- Heart rate slows
- Blood pressure drops
- Emotional stability increases

By controlling your breath, you control your nervous system and can actively switch between the SNS (stress) and the PNS (relaxation). Normally, your nervous system dictates your breathing – fast and shallow in stress, slow and deep in relaxation. But here's the cool part: it's a two-way street. Just as the SNS and PNS influence your breath, you can flip the switch by using your breath to consciously control your nervous system.

The diaphragm, a dome-shaped muscle below your lungs, powers each breath. Often called the 'body's second heart', it contracts during inhalation, expanding the chest cavity and creating a vacuum that pulls air in.[40] When it relaxes, the chest cavity shrinks, allowing air to flow out. Unlike your heart, the diaphragm is unique because it can be automatically and consciously controlled. By intentionally engaging the diaphragm, you can influence more than just airflow; you can tap into your body's natural mechanisms to enhance focus and serenity.

THE VAGUS NERVE: YOUR BUILT-IN STRESS REGULATOR

Your vagus nerve is your body's built-in stress-reset button. Running from your brainstem to your gut, it controls stress responses, immune function and emotional resilience.

When you breathe deeply, your diaphragm movement stimulates the vagus nerve, shifting your body from 'fight or flight' to 'rest and digest'. Your heart rate decreases, blood pressure drops, and your entire system starts to relax. But this isn't just about feeling calmer, it's about resetting your nervous system so your brain can function at its peak.

Struggling to focus? Your breath might be the problem. Deep, controlled breaths flood your brain with oxygen, sharpening memory, boosting concentration and helping you stay cool under pressure. Think of it like filling up your brain's energy tank. Without sufficient oxygen, focusing, learning and even remembering information becomes a struggle.

When we encounter stress, the body's sympathetic nervous system initiates the 'fight or flight' response, increasing our heart rate and alertness. However, the vagus nerve provides a counterbalance to this. By stimulating the vagus nerve through deep breathing, you activate your parasympathetic nervous system. This calming influence is measured as vagal tone, a term reflecting the health and responsiveness of the vagus nerve. Higher vagal tone is linked to improved immune function, emotional regulation and greater overall wellbeing.

The good news? You can train and strengthen your vagus nerve just like a muscle. Simple habits like slow diaphragmatic breathing, cold water therapy, and even humming can significantly improve vagal tone and help you stay cool under pressure.[41]

COLD WATER THERAPY: THE ULTIMATE RESET

Have you ever felt that instant shock from jumping into freezing water? Your breath catches, your heart races, your body panics. That's your nervous system reacting to stress. But what if you could train it to stay calm?

Wim Hof, aka The Iceman, has mastered this. His breathwork techniques allow him to control his nervous system under extreme conditions – scaling icy mountains in shorts, holding world records for cold endurance, and training others to push past mental and physical limits. He advocates cold water therapy as a means to harness the body's natural response mechanisms.[42] His secret? **The breath.**

When you master your breath, you master your body's stress response. Controlled breathing signals your nervous system that you're safe, helping you stay calm and focused, even in high-pressure situations.

Want to try it yourself? Start small:

- **Cold showers:** Begin with 30 seconds of cold water at the end of your shower. Gradually increase the time.

- **Deep breathing:** Try the Wim Hof Method – inhale deeply, exhale fully, repeat 30 times, then hold your breath for as long as comfortable.

- **Stay consistent:** Over time, your body adapts, and what once felt unbearable becomes energising.

Cold water therapy isn't just about physical endurance – it's about reprogramming your mind to handle stress better. Are you up for the challenge?

HARNESSING YOUR BREATH

Studies show that breathing at a rate of about six breaths per minute significantly improves vagal tone, enhancing your body's ability to shift between stress and relaxation.

When you breathe deeply and rhythmically, you send a powerful signal to your brain that you are safe. In response, your body relaxes and your heart rate variability (HRV) – the variation in time between heartbeats – increases. A high HRV is a marker of a flexible, adaptive nervous system, capable of quickly switching between states of alertness and calm. Over time, this practice makes it easier for your body to return to a state of calm after stress, acting as a natural buffer against the demands and pressures of university life. Your breath is your secret weapon against everyday overwhelm.

In addition to physical relaxation, stimulating the vagus nerve through breathwork has a big impact on your emotional wellbeing. The vagus nerve connects to areas in the brain involved in emotional processing, such as the amygdala and prefrontal cortex. When activated through deep breathing, the vagus nerve regulates these brain areas, promoting emotional stability. This is why people with stronger vagal tone tend to be better at managing stress, handling complex emotions and recovering from setbacks.

BUILDING RESILIENCE THROUGH BREATH: PRACTICAL IMPLICATIONS FOR UNIVERSITY LIFE

Understanding the power of the vagus nerve can transform how you approach stress at university. Knowing that you can influence your body's stress response in real time provides a sense of control, even in the face of intense pressure. When preparing for exams, dealing with social situations, or navigating the general stresses of university life, using your breath to engage the vagus nerve helps you stay calm, cool and collected.

Imagine yourself giving a presentation or taking a test. Stress jumbles your thoughts, but by taking a few deep breaths, you can slow down your mind and organise your thoughts. Breathing reminds your brain that you're in control, allowing you to handle high-stress moments with a clearer mind and stable outlook.

So next time you're feeling overwhelmed, close your eyes, breathe in for four, hold for four, exhale for four, and repeat. In just a few cycles, you will find you're thinking clearly, feeling calmer, and ready to tackle whatever comes your way.

CONTROLLED BREATHING AND STRESS REDUCTION

In addition to improving HRV, controlled breathing reduces cortisol. Chronically high levels of cortisol contribute to weakened immunity, sleep disturbances and mental health challenges like anxiety and depression. Research demonstrates that deep, controlled breathing – especially diaphragmatic breathing – can lower cortisol levels in minutes.

One study found that participants who practised deep breathing had significantly lower cortisol levels than those who didn't.[43] Researchers observed that slowing the breath sends calming signals to the brain, which then reduces cortisol release. This is why it's often used in therapy and stress management. There is a direct, measurable impact on the body's stress response.

EMMA WATSON: USING BREATHWORK TO MANAGE STRESS

Imagine juggling a Hollywood career, Ivy League studies and global fame. That was Emma Watson's reality at Brown University. Overwhelmed by stress, she turned to breathing techniques as her secret weapon to stay focused and grounded.

Whenever she felt overwhelmed, Emma would pause, close her eyes, and focus on her breathing. By taking slow, deep breaths, she could calm her mind, reduce anxiety, and stay present. This simple practice became an integral part of her routine, enabling her to navigate high-pressure situations with confidence.

BREATH AS AN ACADEMIC TOOL

Studies show that deep breathing increases alpha brain waves, the same brain activity associated with focus, creativity and flow state. That's why mindfulness and breathwork are being incorporated into high-performance training for surgeons, CEOs and elite athletes.

Next time you're in the library or sitting at your desk, feeling like you're hitting a wall, remember: your breath is right there, ready to help you reset and keep going. With just a few mindful breaths, you're giving yourself a natural boost – no coffee needed.

THE EFFECTS OF BREATH ON PAIN PERCEPTION

Participants who practised slow breathing during a painful experience reported less discomfort than those who didn't.[44] Researchers suggest that the calming effects of slow breathing on the nervous system also lowers pain sensitivity. This connection between breathing and pain relief has led to the use of breathing techniques in medical settings, from childbirth and physical therapy to cancer treatment. By calming the body's stress response, slow breathing offers a natural, drug-free method of pain management.

RESEARCH AND THE FUTURE OF BREATH SCIENCE

While breathing research continues to emerge, scientists are excited about its potential for health. Advances in technology allow researchers to measure the impact of breathing on the body with more accuracy, leading to new insights into breath science. Biofeedback devices, for example, help people learn to control their breathing in real time, providing instant feedback that improves HRV, reduces stress and enhances overall wellbeing.

In the future, we may see breathing techniques as standard components of treatment plans for conditions ranging from anxiety and depression to high blood pressure and chronic pain. Each new study adds weight to the concept of 'breathing as medicine', reinforcing its role as a powerful, non-invasive health tool. But you don't need to wait; you can use this powerful tool now.

Your breath is your hidden superpower, the fastest way to reset your body, mind and energy. No equipment. No cost. Just you, your breath, and the power to change how you feel in seconds. So next time stress hits, before you reach for caffeine, before you spiral into overthinking, just breathe. And watch how everything shifts.

CHAPTER 5:

THE UNSEEN CONSEQUENCES OF POOR BREATHING

'The downside is that the worse our breathing habits are, the closer we are to our own death.'

Anders Olsson

It's mid-afternoon. You're in a lecture hall, struggling to concentrate. Your brain feels foggy. Your breath is shallow. Your shoulders are tense. You feel exhausted, even though you've barely moved. You sigh, reaching for another energy drink, hoping for a jolt of energy. But the real problem isn't caffeine withdrawal or burnout, it's how you're breathing.

You probably never think about your breath, it happens automatically, right? But what if I told you that most people are breathing wrong? In fact, journalist James Nestor found that '99% of people breathe dysfunctionally'[45] without even realising it.

The problem isn't with you, it's cultural. The way we sit, work, study and even eat has hijacked our breathing, shifting it from something that fuels our bodies to something that depletes our energy and resilience. In this chapter, we'll uncover the hidden costs of poor breathing and the simple changes that can transform your focus, energy and stress levels. Breathing is the most powerful yet overlooked tool for wellbeing.

HOW HAS MODERN LIFE BROKEN OUR BREATHING

Let's compare two very different lives, one shaped by nature, the other by modern habits. Kofi, a hunter from Mesolithic Britain (9000 BC), and Sarah, a university student in modern England (2025 AD), could not live more different lives, yet their bodies are designed to function in the same way.

Kofi lives in a world where survival depends on alertness, speed and clear-headed decision-making. He tracks animals across miles of rugged terrain, navigating forests and rivers with skill and precision. His tribe relies on him to bring back food, so his body must perform efficiently, using oxygen to fuel his muscles, keep his senses sharp, and regulate his stress response. His breathing is deep and steady, flowing naturally through his nose, expanding his lungs, and fully engaging his diaphragm. When he senses danger, his breathing quickens, triggering his sympathetic nervous system to prepare him for action. But as soon as the threat passes, his breathing slows, activating his parasympathetic nervous system, allowing his body to relax and recover.

Now, let's shift to Sarah. Her challenges are different, but the pressure feels just as intense. Instead of tracking animals, she's tracking deadlines, exams and social obligations. She's not sprinting through forests; she's hunched over her laptop in a library, sitting for hours on end, shoulders tight, mind racing. Unlike Kofi, her stress has no obvious release. Instead of short bursts of physical exertion followed by rest, her nervous system is locked in a low-level state of fight-or-flight, simmering beneath the surface all day.

Sarah's breathing is shallow and rapid, and trapped high in her chest. Without realising it, she is in a constant state of physiological stress, her body bracing for a threat that never quite arrives. Her brain perceives every unread email, every notification, every upcoming deadline as a potential danger, triggering tension that never fully subsides. Over time, this drains her energy, fogs her thinking and makes focus harder to sustain.

Though their environments couldn't be more different, both Kofi and Sarah rely on their breath to manage stress and stay sharp. The difference? Kofi's natural cycles of movement and breathwork reset his nervous system daily. Sarah, on the other hand, is stuck in a loop of shallow breathing and lingering tension, unable to fully engage the relaxation response that her body is wired to use. Modern life has turned us into dysfunctional breathers.

DISCONNECTED FROM OUR BREATH

Thousands of years ago, deep, rhythmic breathing was instinctive. Our ancestors used their diaphragms fully, drawing oxygen into the lower lungs, optimising their endurance, regulating their stress levels, and sharpening their focus in high-stakes situations.

Today, we are completely disconnected from this natural rhythm. Sedentary lifestyles, chronic stress and even changes in facial structure have fundamentally altered the way we breathe. Anthropologists like Sandra Kahn and Paul Ehrlich have found that, over generations, human jaws have narrowed due to softer diets that require less chewing. This small but significant shift has led to smaller airways, more mouth breathing, and increased rates of respiratory issues. Nasal breathing, which once came naturally, has become more difficult for many people, forcing them into patterns of shallow, inefficient breathing.[46] Beyond structural changes, modern environments present additional challenges.

Think about how much time you spend sitting – whether it's in a lecture hall, at a desk or scrolling on your phone. Sitting for hours encourages slouching, which compresses the chest and abdomen, restricting the movement of the diaphragm. Instead of expanding fully, your lungs are forced into a shallow, upper-chest breathing pattern, starving your body of the oxygen it needs to function at its best. Over time, this low-level restriction drains your energy, increases tension, and reinforces stress patterns in the nervous system.

Air pollution, allergens and indoor heating systems contribute to chronic nasal congestion, making mouth breathing the default for many. Even tight-fitting clothing, like restrictive waistbands, can limit diaphragmatic movement, further encouraging shallow chest breathing.

And then there's technology. Ever caught yourself holding your breath while scrolling on your phone? This is known as screen apnea[47] – a stress response where your body unconsciously limits oxygen intake while staring at a screen. Each time you hold your breath while scrolling, your body reinforces a stress loop. Your brain receives signals that you're in a mild threat state, keeping cortisol elevated and reducing oxygen flow to the prefrontal cortex. The more often this happens, the more your brain wires itself to associate screen time with low-level stress, even when you're just relaxing.[48]

THE HIDDEN IMPACT OF MOUTH BREATHING

One of the most damaging shifts in modern breathing habits is the rise of mouth breathing. While it might seem harmless, studies have linked mouth breathing to increased anxiety, asthma, learning difficulties and even changes in brain function.[49]

Research has found that up to **75% of children with ADHD also have sleep-disordered breathing**, a condition often linked to mouth breathing during sleep. This disrupts the delivery of oxygen to the prefrontal cortex, the area of the brain responsible for focus, decision-making and impulse control.[50]

But this doesn't just affect children. In adults, habitual mouth breathing reduces oxygen intake, increases stress and disrupts sleep cycles, making it harder to concentrate, regulate emotions, and recover from daily mental exertion. The fix? Close your mouth. Breathe through your nose. It's that simple.

Nasal vs. Mouth Breathing

Breathing through your nose does more than just filter air. It warms, humidifies and regulates oxygen intake, creating the ideal conditions for optimal brain function. It also releases nitric oxide, a powerful molecule that widens blood vessels, improves circulation, and enhances oxygen delivery to the brain. More oxygen means better mental clarity, faster thinking and stronger focus, something every student can benefit from.[51]

Mouth breathing, on the other hand, disrupts this natural filtration system, forcing unprocessed air directly into the lungs. Over time, this leads to higher stress levels, increased fatigue and reduced cognitive performance.[52]

THE REAL COST OF POOR BREATHING

Most people assume that the key to better breathing is taking in more oxygen, but carbon dioxide (CO_2) tolerance is just as important. CO_2 plays a crucial role in allowing oxygen to be properly delivered to the brain and muscles. When you breathe too fast or too shallowly – especially through your mouth – you expel too much CO_2. This makes it harder for oxygen to be released into your bloodstream and delivered where it's needed. The result? Brain fog, fatigue and heightened anxiety. Learning to slow your breath and build CO_2 tolerance can significantly improve focus, endurance and emotional resilience.

When your breathing is inefficient, your body suffers. Without adequate oxygen, you feel physically and mentally drained. Research suggests that dysfunctional breathing patterns are linked to increased symptoms of depression, disrupted circadian rhythms, and elevated cortisol levels.

A study found that participants who practised controlled breathing techniques reported greater emotional stability and adaptability.[53] In contrast, those who engaged in shallow, rapid breathing experienced more intense stress responses, even to minor challenges.

Even slight drops in oxygen levels can impair cognitive function, slow processing speed, and make it harder to retain information.[54] This can be particularly frustrating during long study sessions or back-to-back lectures, where even small tasks feel overwhelming. Instead of absorbing information, your mind jumps between thoughts, struggling to stay engaged. And it doesn't stop at mental performance. Shallow breathing also weakens the immune system, making you more vulnerable to illnesses, especially during exam season, when stress is at its peak.

THE HIDDEN IMPACT ON SLEEP & FOCUS

How you breathe during the day influences how you breathe at night. If you spend all day breathing shallowly, your body carries this pattern into sleep, making it harder to enter deep, restorative rest. The body relies on slow, steady breathing to transition into deep sleep. But when you breathe rapidly, even unconsciously, it signals mild stress, keeping your nervous system in a more alert state. This not only reduces the time you spend in deep sleep but can also lead to more frequent wake-ups and restless sleep patterns.

Studies show that poor breath control reduces time spent in rapid eye movement (REM) and deep sleep, leading to fragmented rest, grogginess and impaired memory formation. Poor breathing habits are also linked to sleep disorders like sleep apnea, which disrupts restorative sleep cycles. Many people who suffer from sleep apnea experience heightened fatigue, difficulty focusing, and increased mood disturbances, making academic life even more challenging. Poor breathing isn't just costing you energy today; it's silently stealing your focus, rest, and resilience for tomorrow.

CHAPTER 6:

BREATHWORK FOR SUCCESS

> ### 'Poor breathing is to low energy what a clogged air filter is to bad car performance.'
>
> *Sukhraj S. Dhillon*

You take over 20,000 breaths a day. Each one is an opportunity to reset, refocus and reclaim control. When you master your breath, you master your mind, your energy and your future.

This chapter gives you science-backed breathwork hacks – each one simple, effective and backed by ancient wisdom and modern research.

Hack #1:
DIAPHRAGMATIC (BELLY) BREATHING – UNLOCK YOUR FULL LUNG CAPACITY & REDUCE STRESS

Why It Works

Most people breathe too fast, too shallow and from the chest, keeping their body stuck in a state of low-level stress. Shallow breathing triggers the release of more stress hormones and reduces oxygen to your brain. Deep belly breathing promotes instant calm, sharper focus and more energy.

How to Do It

1. Sit or lie down comfortably.
2. Place one hand on your chest and the other on your belly.
3. Inhale deeply through your nose, feeling your belly expand (not your chest).

4. Exhale slowly through your mouth, feeling your belly fall.

5. Repeat for 5 minutes.

QUICK WIN

Before studying, take 5 belly breaths; it'll instantly boost focus and reduce mental fog.

Next Steps Add 5–10 minutes of belly breathing morning and night for better sleep and stress control.

Research Insight Diaphragmatic breathing lowers cortisol, reduces stress and improves memory retention.[55]

Hack #2:
NASAL BREATHING – YOUR BRAIN'S BEST FRIEND FOR FOCUS & RELAXATION

Why It Works

Breathing through your mouth lowers your brain's oxygen supply.

Mouth breathing leads to poor focus, increased anxiety, and disrupted sleep. Nasal breathing supports clearer thinking, stronger memory, and a healthier immune system.

Nasal breathing filters, warms and humidifies air, ensuring optimal oxygen uptake. It also increases nitric oxide production, which improves circulation and brain function.

How To Do It

1. Breathe in and out only through your nose, especially during workouts. This optimises oxygen intake, improves lung function and enhances endurance.

2. At night, try taping your mouth shut (yes, really, but don't worry, it's not as scary as it sounds). Use medical tape like Micropore, placing a small vertical strip down the centre of your lips. This helps train nasal breathing, leading to better sleep and improved focus.

3. Check your posture; hunched shoulders restrict airflow.

QUICK WIN

Tonight, try taping your mouth shut while sleeping, you'll wake up feeling clear-headed and more refreshed.

Next Steps Make nasal breathing your default. Train yourself to rely on it during situations from studying to physical activity.

Research Insight Nasal breathing enhances cognitive function and reduces anxiety compared to mouth breathing.[56]

Hack #3:
COLD SHOWERS + BREATHWORK – ENERGISE AND BUILD RESILIENCE

Why It Works

Cold exposure triggers deep inhales, activating the sympathetic nervous system, but controlling your breath during cold exposure trains stress resilience. Think you can handle 30 seconds of ice-cold water?

How to Do It

1. Take a normal shower

2. At the end, switch to cold water for the last 30 seconds.

3. Not ready for an icy blast? Start with lukewarm water and gradually turn it colder. Over time, your body will adapt, and so will your resilience.

4. Focus on slow, deep breaths instead of reacting to the cold

QUICK WIN

Tomorrow, end your shower with 30 seconds of cold water, you'll feel alert and energised instantly.

Next Steps Once you've nailed the Level 1, the 30-second blast, it's time to turn up the challenge:

Level 2: Increase to 1 minute, focus on nasal breathing the entire time.

Level 3: Alternate hot and cold: 60 seconds hot, then 60 seconds cold, repeat x3.

Level 4: Full cold shower (no warm water at all), aim for 2–3 minutes.

Level 5: Add box breathing (inhale–hold–exhale–hold for 4 seconds each) to train calm under pressure.

Pick a song you love that's around 2–3 minutes long. Blast it during your cold shower and focus on your breath, not the chill.

You're not just getting clean, you're rewiring your brain to handle discomfort, stress and change with control.

Research Insight Cold exposure, when combined with deep, conscious breathing (like WimHof–style), has been shown to reduce inflammation, boost noradrenaline, and build stress resilience.[57]

STUDENT THRIVE MODE

Hack #4:
THE 4-7-8 TECHNIQUE – THE FASTEST WAY TO FALL ASLEEP & CALM ANXIETY

Need a quick reset before an important exam or an interview? Use 4-7-8 breathing for instant calm. Do three rounds to steady your nerves and sharpen your focus.

Why It Works

This technique slows your heart rate and calms your nervous system, making it perfect for sleep and anxiety relief.

How To Do It

1. Inhale through your nose for 4 seconds.
2. Hold your breath for 7 seconds.
3. Exhale completely through your mouth for 8 seconds.
4. Repeat 4–6 times.

QUICK WIN
Tonight try this in bed – you'll fall asleep faster than ever.

Next Steps Practise this nightly for a week, tracking any improvements in sleep quality and relaxation.

Research Insight The 4-7-8 breathing method activates the parasympathetic nervous system, which lowers cortisol, reduces heart rate, and promotes relaxation.[58]

Hack #5:
HUMMING BREATH – ACTIVATE YOUR VAGUS NERVE & ENHANCE RELAXATION

Why It Works

Humming stimulates the vagus nerve, which promotes calmness and relaxation.

How To Do It

1. Inhale deeply through your nose.

2. Exhale while humming softly, focusing on the sound and vibration.

3. Repeat for 2–3 minutes.

QUICK WIN

Feeling anxious? Humming breath will calm you down instantly.

Next Steps Make humming breath a daily habit by adding it to your morning or evening routine, just 3 minutes a day can train your body to switch into calm mode more quickly over time.

Research Insight Humming increases nitric oxide levels in the nasal passages, which plays a vital role in supporting lung function and relaxation.[59]

Hack #6:

ALTERNATE NOSTRIL BREATHING – BALANCE BRAIN FUNCTION & FOCUS

Why It Works

This ancient yogic technique balances both sides of the brain, improving focus and emotional regulation.

How To Do It

1. Close your right nostril with your thumb, and inhale through the left nostril.

2. Switch nostrils, exhaling through the right.

3. Inhale through the right, then switch and exhale through the left.

4. Repeat for 5–10 minutes.

QUICK WIN

Use this between study sessions to feel recharged and mentally sharp.

Next Steps Use this technique twice a day for better mental clarity and balance.

Research Insight Alternate nostril breathing (also called Nadi Shodhana) improves cognitive performance, including attention, reaction time, and memory.[60]

Hack #7:

THE PHYSIOLOGICAL SIGH – THE QUICKEST STRESS RELIEVER

Why It Works This quick reset triggers the parasympathetic nervous system, lowering stress and tension.

How To Do It

1. Take one deep inhale through your nose.

2. Follow it with a second, shorter inhale to fully expand your lungs.

3. Exhale slowly and entirely through your mouth.

4. Repeat 2–3 times.

QUICK WIN

Feeling overwhelmed in the middle of a test? About to step on stage for a presentation? Use the physiological sigh to reset your nervous system in seconds and regain control.

Next Steps Make this a go-to stress management tool, practising daily.

Research Insight Neuroscientists have found that the physiological sigh significantly reduces stress and improves relaxation by balancing oxygen and CO_2 levels.[61]

Hack #8:
BREATH COUNTING – A SIMPLE MEDITATION HACK FOR FOCUS & CLARITY

Why It Works A simple technique to focus the mind and train attention.

How To Do It

1. Sit comfortably, close your eyes and take a deep breath.

2. On your exhale, count 'one'.

3. Inhale, then exhale, count 'two'.

4. Continue up to ten, then start over if you get distracted, maintaining awareness of each breath.

QUICK WIN

Practise breath counting for 5 minutes to ground yourself before a stressful task.

Next Steps Build this into a daily mindfulness practice, gradually extending your time to 10–15 minutes.

Research Insight Breath-focused meditation has been linked to enhanced focus, emotional regulation and resilience to stress.[62]

Hack #9:
THE WIM HOF METHOD – OXYGENATE, ENERGISE AND BUILD RESILIENCE

Why It Works The Wim Hof Method combines deep breathing with breath retention to restore physical and mental balance.

How To Do it

1. Sit comfortably and take 30–40 deep breaths, inhaling and exhaling fully.

2. After the last exhale, hold your breath as long as comfortable.

3. Breathe in deeply to recover, holding for 15 seconds.

4. Release.

5. Repeat the cycle 2–3 times.

QUICK WIN

Try a round of the Wim Hof Method in the morning for an energising start to your day.

Next Steps Practise three rounds, 3x per week.

Research Insight The Wim Hof Method improves oxygen efficiency, reduce inflammation and enhance resilience.[63]

Hack #10:
RESONANT BREATHING – THE ULTIMATE NERVOUS SYSTEM RESET FOR PEAK PERFORMANCE

Why It Works

Resonant breathing is one of the most studied breathwork techniques in performance psychology. It fine-tunes your nervous system, optimises heart rate variability (HRV) and increases cognitive function, memory and stress tolerance.

It isn't just a wellness trick, it's a science-backed tool used by professional athletes, CEOs and high-level performers to maintain laser focus and composure under pressure.

Studies show that resonant breathing can:

- Reduce anxiety
- Improve cognitive function and memory
- Enhance emotional resilience and heart rate variability (HVR)

How To Do It

1. Inhale through your nose for 5 seconds.

2. Exhale through your nose for 5 seconds.

3. Maintain this smooth, rhythmic pattern for 5 minutes.

4. Keep your breaths equal in length to create a steady, calming rhythm.

Why 5 seconds? Breathing at this rhythm (around 5 breaths per minute) optimises oxygen delivery, balances the nervous system and promotes mental clarity.

QUICK WIN

Before an exam, presentation or stressful moment, practise 5 minutes of resonant breathing to reset your focus and enter a state of calm, sharp awareness.

Next Steps

Before studying, do 10 minutes of resonant breathing for sharper concentration.

Research Insight Resonant breathing has been shown to enhance emotional regulation, reduce anxiety and improve HRV, a key marker of nervous system balance and resilience[64].

Breathe Your Way to Peak Performance

Your breath is your superpower, no equipment, no cost, just pure control over your body and mind. **Pick just ONE hack today and try it.** Whether it's a deep belly breath before studying or a physiological sigh in a stressful moment, one breath can change everything.

PILLAR 3:

MOVE

UNLOCK ENERGY, FOCUS & STRENGTH

THROUGH MOVEMENT

CHAPTER 7:

BUILT TO MOVE

'Walking is man's best medicine.'

Hippocrates

Picture your typical day at university. Lectures. Coffee breaks. Study sessions. Netflix. Most of it? Sitting. Maybe you walk between classes or hit the gym once or twice a week. But, for most students, movement feels like an 'extra', something to squeeze in when you can, a box to tick rather than a core part of life. Sound familiar? Now imagine if movement was as essential as breathing. Spoiler: it is.

Movement is in our DNA. Our muscles and brains are designed for it.[65] For most of human history, movement wasn't optional – it was survival. Our ancestors didn't need gyms or step counters. Movement was life, and it shaped our body and mind.

Today, movement has faded from our daily routines. This is a problem because movement is nature's antidepressant, focus enhancer and stress reset button. We're built to move, not just to survive but to thrive.

TWO LIVES, 10,000 YEARS APART

Meet Koma, a prehistoric woman, and Jess, a university student in Edinburgh. Koma's life was movement. She walked miles for water, climbed for fruit, and carried her home across vast landscapes, adapting to seasonal changes and following animal migrations to remain fed. Every step released brain-boosting chemicals, dopamine for focus, serotonin for mood, and endorphins for comfort, keeping her sharp, motivated and well-rested.

Jess, on the other hand, wakes to a blaring alarm, scrolls her phone, and spends her day sitting in lectures and cafes. Her world discourages movement, leaving her groggy, unfocused and restless.

Stress floods her system like Koma facing a predator, but without an outlet, it lingers, disrupting her sleep and energy. The difference? Koma's brain rewarded movement. Jess's brain is confused.

MOVEMENT MATTER: EXERCISE VS. DAILY ACTIVITY

So, what can we learn from the contrast between Koma's active life and Jess's sedentary one? For one, there's a difference between exercise and movement.

> ### THE DIFFERENCE BETWEEN EXERCISE AND MOVEMENT
>
> **Exercise** is intentional, running, lifting weights or swimming. It's structured and goal-orientated.
>
> **Movement** is everything else: walking, stretching, carrying groceries, fidgeting. All exercise is movement, but not all movement is exercise, yet both are essential.

Koma's life was filled with movement unconfined by a gym or workout session. Her physicality was a by-product of an active lifestyle. Jess has to intentionally fit movement into her modern, convenience-driven world.

Anthropologists estimate that early humans walked anywhere from 6 to 12 miles a day, engaging in moderate to intense physical exertion over extended periods.[66] This consistent activity shaped our physiology in lasting ways. For example, our long limbs and upright posture are optimised for efficient walking and running, while sweat glands cool us down. This is in contrast to many other mammals, who rely on panting or have limited endurance capabilities. But now?

We've engineered movement out of our lives. The average student walks less than 2 miles a day. And it's making us sicker, more stressed and less focused than ever before. This drastic shift is rewiring our brains and bodies in ways we were never designed for.

THE PSYCHOLOGICAL PERKS OF MOVING

When was the last time you sprinted across campus to make it to a lecture or climbed a flight of stairs because the lift was broken? You probably didn't think much of it, but your brain did. Every movement, no matter how small, has a powerful impact on your mind. And the best part? You don't need a gym membership or intense workouts to reap the benefits. Here's how.

THE BRAIN BOOSTING BENEFITS OF MOVEMENT

1. Movement is a Natural Performance Enhancer

One of the biggest perks of movement? How it makes you feel. Physical activity triggers the release of serotonin and endorphins – the body's 'feel-good' chemicals.

But there's another key player: endocannabinoids, the body's natural compounds that act on the same receptors as cannabis. These molecules, particularly anandamide, contribute to the 'runner's high', a sense of euphoria, reduced stress and enhanced mood. Unlike endorphins, which are too large to cross the blood-brain barrier, endocannabinoids are small enough to have a direct effect on your nervous system, making you feel calmer and more focused after exercise. But you don't have to run a marathon to experience it.[67] Even a short walk or a few minutes of stretching can trigger anandamide release, helping to improve your mood and reduce anxiety.

When you exercise, your brain also releases dopamine, which plays a crucial role in sustaining focus and motivation. A brisk walk or stretching can provide more mental clarity and drive than another cup of coffee or scroll through TikTok. Meanwhile, serotonin, often called the body's natural 'anti-depressant',[68] helps regulate mood. Movement supports the balance between dopamine and serotonin, known as the 'dopamine-serotonin loop', ensuring we stay driven towards our goals while feeling rewarded along the way.[69]

Research using MRI scans shows that even brief periods of physical activity improve brain function, enhance neuroplasticity and boost overall cognitive performance.[70]

2. Movement Acts Like a Stress-Reset Button

When you're stressed, your body produces cortisol and triggers the fight-or-flight response. Movement is like a reset button for your body's stress system. Physical activity 'uses up' cortisol, helping it dissipate. It also activates the body's HPA (hypothalamic-pituitary-adrenal) axis, a part of the brain that manages stress by regulating hormone levels.[71]

Your brain has a system that keeps stress in check, and the amygdala is constantly scanning for threats. When the amygdala senses danger, it sounds an alert, releasing cortisol. While this is useful in risky situations, the amygdala can overreact, causing spirals of stress and anxiety that can lead to panic. Fortunately, the hippocampus (another part of the brain) acts as a brake on these stress signals.

Regular movement strengthens the hippocampus, teaching it that not every increase in heart rate or blood pressure means panic, but also excitement or positive emotions. Over time, exercise can recalibrate its responses, reducing the likelihood of overreacting.

In a way, movement helps the amygdala and hippocampus communicate. After exercise, cortisol levels temporarily spike before dropping below pre-exercise levels. Over time, consistent activity regulates stress effectively, which would help Jess remain cool under pressure. And the result? More resilience. Less anxiety. Even low-intensity movement, like walking or stretching, helps reset your stress response.

3. Movement Supercharges Brainpower

Movement makes you smarter. Every time you move, your brain releases BDNF (brain-derived neurotrophic factor), a protein which plays a major role in supporting memory and learning.[72] It encourages the birth of neurons and strengthens existing connections.

MRI studies have shown that after 20–30 minutes of movement, your brain produces more BDNF, giving you a cognitive boost.[73] In contrast, sitting for too long has the opposite effect. Inactivity increases inflammation, dulls focus and limits blood flow to the brain.

It doesn't take a gym membership to start doing this. A short walk, stretching or a few minutes of dancing makes a difference. Studies have shown that students recall up to 20% more words when listening to them while walking compared to sitting still. So, if you're prepping for exams, walk while listening to notes or study while standing, it's a brain hack that works.

Here's how regular movement supercharges your brain health:

- **Increased blood flow**: Movement delivers oxygen and nutrients to the brain.

- **Release of growth factors**: Movement boosts neurotrophins.

- **Lowered Stress Hormones**: Physical activity reduces cortisol.

- **Enhanced Neuroplasticity**: Moving encourages brain flexibility.

- **Better Sleep and Mood**: Movement improves bodily functions.

- **Reduced Inflammation**: Neurons thrive without pressure.

4. Movement is a Natural Prescription without Side Effects

Movement is medicine. When it comes to lifting your mood, movement may be one of the best 'prescriptions' available and it comes without a single side effect. Research proves that physical activity offers powerful protection against depression.[74] Psychologist James Blumenthal found that regular exercise was as effective as, if not better than, antidepressants for treating mild to moderate depression.[75]

THE PHYSICAL BENEFITS OF MOVING

1. Stronger Bones and Muscles The musculoskeletal system, bones, muscles and joints, gives us the ability to move. It depends on physical activity to remain strong. Bones, for instance, respond to movement through a process called 'bone remodelling'.[76] Weight-bearing exercises such as walking, running, and lifting stimulate cells to create new bone tissue. Breakdown and renewal are essential for maintaining bone density and preventing conditions like osteoporosis, which can lead to fractures and limited mobility.

When we engage in strength-training exercises like lifting weights or bodyweight resistance, our muscles experience tiny tears that repair and grow stronger. This improves muscle mass and supports balance and posture. In addition to their physical strength benefits, muscles play a vital role in metabolic health.

Joints benefit significantly from regular activity. Physical activity stimulates the production of synovial fluid, which acts as a lubricant, reducing friction and preventing stiffness.[77]

2. A Healthier Heart & Lungs Moving, even a walk to class, gets your heart pumping, delivering oxygen and nutrients throughout your body. Over time, this boosts energy, helping you power through classes, study marathons and nights out. Cardio exercises like running, cycling and swimming strengthen your heart and improve circulation.

Your lungs benefit, too! Aerobic activity increases oxygen flow, enhances lung capacity, and reduces fatigue. With a stronger heart and lungs, your body works more efficiently, so you feel better, longer. Beyond immediate benefits, cardiovascular exercises regulate cholesterol levels, reducing 'bad' LDL cholesterol while increasing 'good' HDL cholesterol.[78] This balance is crucial for heart health, as high levels of LDL cholesterol lead to plaque buildup in the arteries.

3. Less Cravings Move first, eat smarter. Exercise also balances hunger hormones, making you less likely to crave junk food. Research shows that a short walk before eating reduces cravings for sugary, ultra-processed foods.

Your brain isn't looking for sugar, it's looking for dopamine. Move, and it will find it naturally.

4. Better Sleep & Mood Movement reduces anxiety and improves sleep quality by regulating circadian rhythms.

5. Setting Yourself Up for the Future

Staying fit also sets you up for future success. Studies show that physical fitness in your late teens is linked to higher academic achievement and greater job prospects, often with higher salaries by age 40.[79] Being fit in your twenties reduces the risk of developing neurological issues later in life, like epilepsy or dementia. This isn't just about feeling good today. It's about future-proofing your brain, body and success.

Movement as a Life Hack

Here's something most people don't realise: moving more can even make you richer and healthier!

Move More, Spend Less

Studies show that exercise reduces impulsive spending. Why? Because movement naturally regulates dopamine, reducing the need for quick 'hits' from online shopping or takeaway food. The next time you feel the urge to splurge on impulse buys, take a 10-minute walk first. Chances are, the craving will disappear.

Your brain doesn't care that the world no longer looks like the savannah, it remains wired to reward you for movement. By releasing feel-good chemicals like dopamine and serotonin when you are active, you are rewarded for that run, walk or dance session. This response is because your brain interprets movement as an activity that increases your chances of survival.

Extended periods of inactivity signal to your brain that something's wrong, which is why inactivity feels so draining. Want to feel sharper, happier, and more energised? Move.

CHAPTER 8:

THE HIDDEN COST OF SITTING STILL

'Those who think they have no time for exercise will sooner or later have to find time for illness.'

Edward Stanley

Inactivity doesn't conserve energy, it drains it. Sitting all day doesn't make you more focused or productive; it slows you down. Your brain and body weren't designed for this modern experiment.

For most of human history, movement was built into daily life. Now, we've engineered it out. We study, shop and socialise – all from a chair. This leaves us more sedentary than any generation before. Our bodies haven't had the chance to adapt. We're wired to need movement, creating a mismatch that has serious health implications.

This chapter reveals why a sedentary lifestyle is sabotaging your body, mind and academic performance, and what to do about it.

THE SEDENTARY EPIDEMIC: HOW WE GOT HERE

It's almost ironic, isn't it? We pay good money to get back what our ancestors had for free – daily movement. Fitness culture sells us the idea that health requires expensive workouts, high-tech wearables, and curated routines. But movement was never meant to be a luxury; it was life.

We're spectators of others' physical feats, cheering from our couches with pizza and beer as athletes push themselves to the limits. While most of us understand that it's essential, many feel intimidated or unwelcome in fitness spaces. And it's killing us.

The World Health Organisation (WHO) calls physical inactivity one of the top 10 leading causes of death globally. Yet, it's hardly our fault. Our ancestors, just a few generations back, may have worked on farms or in factories, incorporating movement naturally, but now, most of us sit at desks, no longer incorporating movement as our ancestors did. This 'culture of convenience' has consequences that are only just starting to reveal themselves.[80] In Europe, 50% of women and 40% of men fail to get enough exercise.[81]

INACTIVITY: PHYSICAL CONSEQUENCES

How many hours a day do you spend sitting? The average student sits for 9+ hours a day. Studies have linked prolonged sitting to a host of chronic health issues once associated with old age or those with an unhealthy lifestyle. Today, conditions like obesity, heart disease, and mental health disorders are increasingly common in young adults who lead sedentary lives.[82] The worst part? Most of us don't even realise how little we move. Sitting for long hours puts your body into a 'passive' state,[83] leading to:

1. Cardiovascular Damage & Weakened Circulation

Blood circulation slows, muscles weaken, and our metabolism grows sluggish, setting off a series of physical consequences. Your heart is a muscle that needs regular activity to stay strong. Physical movement makes your heart pump faster, strengthening it and keeping your circulatory system in top shape. When you sit for hours, your heart misses out on a much-needed workout. Blood flow slows, and reduced circulation hinders your heart's ability to pump oxygen and nutrients around your body, gradually weakening its muscles.

People who sit for prolonged periods have a higher risk of cardiovascular issues, such as high blood pressure, atherosclerosis (the hardening of the arteries), and even blood clots.[84] While these risks might feel like distant concerns, by the time symptoms show, these conditions have usually been progressing for a long time.

2. Metabolic Slowdown and Weight Gain

When you're inactive, your metabolism (the process by which your body converts food into energy) slows. Physical activity activates metabolism, which is key for maintaining a healthy weight. A sedentary lifestyle reduces the rate at which you burn calories, leading to gradual weight gain. A slow metabolism increases the risk of obesity and type 2 diabetes. Physical movement regulates insulin effectively. Without it, you're more likely to experience blood sugar spikes and crashes, which leave you feeling tired and mentally drained.[85]

3. Muscle Weakness & Poor Posture

Sitting weakens your muscles, particularly those in your core. These support your posture and organs. Tight hip flexors and rounded shoulders are common among students who spend hours hunched over desks or laptops.

Poor posture isn't just uncomfortable; it makes focusing on studies and enjoying activities harder. Over time, this lack of muscle engagement makes movement feel more difficult, as your body isn't conditioned for physical activity.

4. Increased Risk of Chronic Conditions

Prolonged sitting is linked to 35+ chronic diseases, including diabetes, high cholesterol and osteoporosis.[86] But even in young people, not moving enough can lead to stiffness, joint pain and muscle strain, things you might already be feeling during long study sessions or lectures.

But physical health isn't the only thing at stake. The effects of inactivity impact mental wellbeing in ways that are often overlooked. This means that sitting all day doesn't just affect you right now; it sets the stage for irreversible, long-term health challenges.

And it's not just physical health, your mind suffers, too.

5. Anxiety

Inactivity increases cortisol, creating a cycle of heightened stress and low mood. Studies show that sedentary lifestyles correlate with a higher risk of depression and anxiety, two issues many students are all too familiar with.[87] When stress accumulates without an outlet, anxiety builds. Without movement, there's little relief. Regular movement acts like a 'reset' for your mind, helping to maintain emotional balance.[88]

Movement is the natural way to 'use up' cortisol, helping to reduce any lingering effects.[89] It also promotes the release of endorphins, which soothe the body and mind. By prioritising even light movement each day (walking, stretching, dancing), you can protect your mental health, improve academic performance, and support long-term wellbeing.

6. Brain Fog

Have you ever felt sluggish after hours of sitting? This 'brain fog' is your body's way of signalling that it's time to move.[90] Without regular movement, blood flow to your brain slows, sapping your energy and sharpening feelings of stress and anxiety. The more you sit, the harder it becomes to break the cycle. Low energy leads to more sitting, draining you further.

7. Academic Performance

A sedentary lifestyle doesn't just affect physical and mental health; it directly impacts academic performance. Research shows that prolonged inactivity lowers cognitive function, meaning that hours of cramming without breaks may not be as effective as you think.[91] Physical activity increases oxygen flow to the brain, enhancing focus and boosting productivity. Active students outperform sedentary students academically, every time. So, if you're studying for hours without moving, you're not helping yourself.

Want to study smarter? Stand up. Move around. Walk while reviewing notes. It's easy to get caught up in the demands of university life, but making time for movement is one of the best things you can do for yourself.

The fitness industry sells the idea that exercise requires gym memberships, personal trainers, and the latest workout gear. It's easy to feel like you need to spend money to stay active, but that's simply not true. If you enjoy the gym, great. But it's not essential.

Movement doesn't need to be expensive, complicated or tied to consumerism. Koma didn't need a branded fitness tracker to stay active. Jess, on the other hand, feels like exercise is something she has to pay for, when in reality, her body was built to move, no purchase necessary.

To note: Be cautious of expensive nutritional supplements and other miracle products which claim to work wonders for the brain. You don't need to pay a penny; you just need to move.

CHAPTER 9:

EASY WAYS TO STAY ACTIVE AT UNI

> '*Take care of your body. It's the only place you have to live.*'
>
> *Jim Rohn*

Movement is the most powerful, accessible and affordable form of medicine available to us. Yet, in our tech-driven, desk-bound world, it's become optional. We spend hours sitting, studying, scrolling or binge-watching Netflix, forgetting how essential it is to move. We're built to move, and when we don't, it takes its toll, physically, mentally and academically. In this chapter, I will show you how to make movement a seamless part of your university routine. With small, simple actions – like short 'movement snacks' or nature walks – you'll transform your physical and mental performance. Let's get moving!

Hack #1:
WALKING – NATURE'S BRAIN-BOOSTER

Why It Works You might not think of walking as a workout, but it's one of the best ways to move your body. When you walk, your body releases myokines, molecules that make you more resistant to stress and more sensitive to joy. Walking also increases BDNF (brain-derived neurotrophic factor), which helps grow nerve cells and improves memory.[92]

How To Do It

1. Walk to class instead of taking the bus or driving.

2. Schedule 'walk and talk' study sessions with friends.

3. Take a short walk after a meal to aid digestion and stabilise energy.

QUICK WIN

Tomorrow, swap one bus ride for a walk. Feel the fresh air, clear your head, and boost your brainpower before you even step into class.

Next Steps Set a daily step goal (start with 5,000 and work up to 10,000 steps). Walking outside with a friend or while listening to a podcast makes it even more enjoyable.

Research Insight In a landmark study, adults who walked for 40 minutes, three times a week, for a year showed measurable growth in hippocampal volume, alongside improvements in memory and executive function.[93]

Hack #2:
SIT LESS – SMALL SHIFTS, BIG IMPACT

Why It Works Sitting is the new smoking. Long periods of sitting slow your metabolism, weaken muscles and increase stress levels. The good news? Even small changes can make a big difference.

How To Do It

1. Set reminders: Use a timer to remind yourself to stand up and move every 30–45 minutes.

2. Walk while you talk: If you have a call or meeting, stand up or walk around while engaged.

3. Study standing up: Try using a standing desk or stack some books to raise your laptop.

QUICK WIN

Next time you're studying, stand and stretch every 30 minutes. Walk to the kitchen, do a quick lap around your bedroom, or shake out your legs to get the blood flowing.

Next Steps Create 'movement triggers' – stand while drinking tea/coffee, stretch after finishing a chapter, or walk while brainstorming ideas.

Research Insight In controlled trials, participants who stood or moved for just 2–3 minutes every 30 minutes had significantly better blood sugar control compared to those who sat continuously.[94]

Hack #3:
TURN DAILY HABITS INTO FUNCTIONAL FITNESS

Why It Works

Think you don't have time for exercise? Think again. Stacking simple movements onto everyday habits, like brushing your teeth or boiling the kettle, you can sneak in strength and energy boosts without adding to your schedule. These hidden workouts turn routine moments into fitness wins.

How To Do It

1. Do 10 squats while waiting for the kettle to boil.
2. Rise onto your toes for calf raises whilst brushing your teeth.
3. Stretch or twist whilst making lunch or packing your bag.
4. Turn the music up and dance while you tidy your room or are getting dressed.

QUICK WIN

Tomorrow morning, try this: 20 calf raises while brushing your teeth

Next Steps: Keep stacking movement onto existing habits:

- Stretch when you wake up
- Squat while your coffee brews
- Dance while making breakfast
- Calf raises everyday while brushing

The goal is to make movement a natural part of your daily routine.

Research Insight: Short bursts of movement before meals can significantly lower blood sugar levels, helping your body manage food effectively.[95]

Hack #4:
STRENGTH TRAINING – BUILD A STRONGER, SHARPER BRAIN

Strength training isn't just for muscles; it enhances brain function, posture and metabolic health.

Why It Works

- **Boosts brain function.** Strength training increases BDNF, which enhances memory and learning.
- **Improves posture & energy.** A strong core reduces fatigue and back pain, keeping you more alert throughout the day.
- **Enhances metabolic health.** More muscle means a higher metabolism, better insulin sensitivity and sustained energy levels.

How To Do It

1. **Bodyweight exercises:** squats, lunges, push-ups, planks and tricep dips are simple exercises you can do without equipment, anywhere.

2. **Functional strength:** Carry heavy groceries or books around campus

3. **Use resistance bands for a quick strength workout:** you really don't need the gym.

QUICK WIN

Try this 5-minute strength workout:

• 10 squats   • 10 push-ups   • 30-second plank

Next Steps: Schedule 2–3 strength-training sessions into your week, even if it's just bodyweight exercises in your bedroom. The stronger your body, the sharper your brain.

Research Insight: A group of young adults (ages 18–30) participated in a weight resistance programme twice a week for 10 weeks. Compared to a group who didn't train, they showed faster thinking, better focus, and improved problem-solving, especially when reading complex information.[96]

Hack #5:
RUN YOUR WAY TO A SHARPER MIND

Why It Works

If you're looking for an activity that boosts your physical and mental health, running is one of the best options. It improves cardiovascular health, significantly affects brain function, and is particularly effective at boosting BDNF levels. [97]

How To Do It

1. Start with short intervals: run for 1 minute, walk for 1 minute, and repeat. Gradually increase your running time.

2. Try the Couch to 5K programme to guide you through a beginner-friendly plan.

3. Aim for 45-minute runs, 3x a week, for maximum brain benefits.

QUICK WIN

This week, lace up your trainers and go for a 10-minute jog. If running sounds daunting, start with a walk and incorporate short bursts of running.

Next Steps: Gradually build up your running routine. Whether it's 20-minute jogs or training for a 5K, running will boost your physical and mental health in a major way. Check out your nearest Park Run https://www.parkrun.org.uk/

Research Insight: Two groups of American students suffering from anxiety were told to either walk or run for 20 minutes several times a week over the course of 2 weeks.[98] Anxiety levels fell for both groups and stayed low for 24 hours, with the effects lasting long after the research concluded.

Hack #6:
NATURE EXPOSURE – MOVE OUTSIDE FOR MAXIMUM BENEFITS

Why it Works

- **Nature is the ultimate stress reliever,** being outside boosts your mood, grounds you, and even improves your focus and creativity. Whether it's a walk in the park or standing by water, simply connecting with nature is a powerful way to improve your wellbeing.

- **Regulates your body clock,** sunlight helps reset your circadian rhythm, improving sleep and energy levels.
- **Enhances brain function,** fresh air and natural surroundings improve focus, mental clarity and cognitive performance more than indoor environments.

How To Do It

1. Schedule weekly walks or hikes in a park or nature reserve.
2. Get outside in the morning for at least 10 minutes to breathe in fresh air.
3. Open windows wherever you can see or hear nature.

QUICK WIN

Tomorrow, take a 15-minute walk before your day starts. Whether it's in a park or just around campus, being in nature will leave you refreshed.

Next Steps Make nature a regular part of your life. Plan weekly outings to green spaces. Eat your lunch outside or even organise study groups in the park. Time spent in nature will clear your mind and boost your academic performance. Listen to nature sounds (even recorded ones) to boost relaxation if you can't get outside.

Research Insight Spending just 15 minutes in nature lowers cortisol levels, boosts endorphins and helps manage stress effectively.[99]

Hack #7:
ACTIVE STUDY BREAKS - BOOST FOCUS AND FIGHT FATIGUE

Why It Works

Movement increases blood flow to the brain, delivering oxygen and nutrients that boost focus, memory and mental clarity. Even short bursts of physical activity reset your nervous system, fight fatigue and make it easier to absorb and retain information.

How To Do It

1. After 30–45 minutes of studying, take a 5-minute movement break.

2. Alternate between sitting and standing while reviewing notes.

3. Pomodoro technique: study for 25 minutes, then take a 5-minute break.

QUICK WIN

During your next study session, set a timer for 30 minutes, and when it goes off, stand and do 10 jumping jacks or a quick stretch. Notice how much more alert you feel afterwards.

Next Steps Make active study breaks a habit by integrating them into your daily routine. Experiment with different activities like stretching, yoga or a short walk between study sessions.

Research Insight Students who engaged in physical activity during revision breaks performed better on memory and recall tests than those who rested passively.[100]

Hack #8:
DANCE IT OUT – BOOST ENERGY AND JOY THROUGH MOVEMENT

Exercise doesn't have to feel like a chore. Dancing is a fun, social way to move your body, release stress and boost your mood.

Why it Works

- **Releases endorphins.** Dancing is proven to reduce stress and increase happiness.

- **Enhances brain function.** It combines physical movement with coordination and rhythm, boosting cognitive performance.

- **Encourages social connection.** Dancing with others strengthens social bonds and increases motivation.

How To Do It

1. Dance to your favourite song while getting ready in the morning.

2. Join a dance class or attend social dancing events on campus.

3. Take a dance break when you're stressed or overwhelmed.

QUICK WIN

Right now, put on a song you love and dance for 3–5 minutes. You'll feel an instant mood boost and increase your energy levels!

Next Steps Turn dance breaks into a daily habit. Whether it's a solo session in your room, a dance class or a night out with friends, make movement a joyful part of your routine.

Research Insight Studies reveal that regular dancing can enhance brain plasticity, slow cognitive decline, and improve learning and attention, especially in young adults and older populations alike. Dancing boosts brain function by combining physical movement, mental coordination and social interaction..[101]

Hack #9:

TAKE THE STAIRS – TURN EVERYDAY STEPS INTO A FITNESS BOOST

Stair climbing isn't just a way to get from one floor to another, it's a workout that strengthens your heart, tones your legs and boosts your metabolism. Best of all, you don't need a gym or fancy equipment. Every staircase is an opportunity to build fitness, one step at a time.

Why It Works

- **Supercharges heart health.** Climbing stairs gets your heart pumping, improving endurance and cardiovascular fitness.

- **Strengthens the lower body.** Activates key muscle groups, including quads, hamstrings, glutes and calves, for stronger, more toned legs.

- **Fires up metabolism.** Helps regulate blood sugar, increases calorie burn and improves overall metabolic function.

- Enhances balance & coordination. Engages core stability, improving posture and agility over time.

How To Do It

1. **Skip the lift, take the stairs.** Build movement into your day by choosing stairs whenever possible.

2. **Stair sprint intervals.** Power walk or jog up a flight of stairs, then walk down. Repeat for 5–10 minutes for a quick cardio blast.

3. **Bodyweight stair exercises.** Use a staircase for calf raises, step-ups or incline push-ups to add variety to your routine.

4. **The 'one more flight' rule.** Challenge yourself to take one extra flight of stairs beyond your usual destination. Small progress leads to big results!

QUICK WIN

Next time you spot a staircase, whether on campus, at work or in a shopping centre, make it your go-to choice. Each step you take is a step towards better health.

Next Steps Set a goal: Dedicate 10 minutes once a week to a stair workout. Try sprinting up, doing bodyweight exercises between flights, or setting a personal record for the number of flights climbed. Track your progress and push yourself a little further each time!

Small steps (literally!) lead to big fitness gains. Ready to take the challenge?

Research Insight A large scale study found that climbing just 8–10 flights of stairs daily can significantly improve heart health and lower the risk of premature mortality. It's a simple yet powerful way to boost fitness with minimal time investment.[102]

Hack #10:
BUDDY UP – BOOST MOTIVATION AND FUN WITH A WORKOUT PARTNER

Why It Works: Exercising with a friend not only makes movement more fun, it also helps keep you accountable. Having a workout partner can motivate you to stay consistent and push yourself further.

How To Do It

1. Plan regular walks, runs or gym sessions with a friend.
2. Join a university sports team or club together.
3. Use social platforms like Strava or MyFitnessPal to track progress and encourage each other.

QUICK WIN

Text a friend today and schedule a walk or workout together. You'll have fun, strengthen your friendship, and stay active all at once.

Next Steps Make social movement a habit. Whether it's a morning run, a study break walk or a fitness class, having a workout buddy keeps you on track and makes exercise more enjoyable.

Research Insight A study from Oxford University found that people who exercise with friends are more likely to stick to their workout routines as they experience higher endorphin levels.[103]

Move for a Healthier Mind and Body

Movement is one of the most powerful performance hacks. It's medicine for your body and brain. Whether it's walking, strength training, or simply standing, every little bit counts. By integrating these simple movement hacks into your daily routine, you'll feel more energised and focused and better equipped to handle university.

Remember, you don't need to spend hours at the gym to see the benefits. Small, consistent actions create lasting change. Start where you are, move a little more each day, and watch how it transforms your physical health, mental clarity and academic performance.

Your challenge: Pick one hack and try it today. See how movement boosts your energy, focus and mood!

PILLAR 4:

FUEL

NOURISH YOUR BODY & MIND FOR

PEAK PERFORMANCE

CHAPTER 10:
UNDERSTANDING NUTRITION

'Each of us has an enormous opportunity to take charge of our lives using food to transform our health.'

Dr. William Li

In a world of viral health trends and influencer endorsements flooding our feeds, it's easy to get drawn into the promise of quick-fix diets. The Ice-Cream Cleanse. The Lion Diet. The Cabbage Soup Diet. The Military Diet with its strange mix of hot dogs and tuna. Some take it even further, replacing meals with jars of baby food or surviving on nothing but steak and salt. They all sound bizarre, yet they have followers convinced they hold the key to effortless weight loss.

Sure, these diets offer structure, follow trends and promise fast results with minimal effort. But here's the catch: they leave you tired, stressed and malnourished. Not only are they unsustainable, but some can be harmful to your health. When you're juggling lectures, revision sessions and a part-time job, your body and mind need real, lasting fuel, not short-term gimmicks.

WHY NUTRITION IS YOUR MOST POWERFUL ACADEMIC TOOL

Fad diets might be fun to read about (or laugh at), but they're not the secret to long-term health. Forget diet trends and calorie counting, what you eat isn't just about how much you weigh. It directly impacts how well your brain and body perform.

Every function in your body, from staying alert in lectures to managing stress and retaining information, depends on proper nutrition. When you eat well, you think faster, focus longer and remember more. On the flip side, poor nutrition leads to sluggishness, poor concentration and low motivation.

HOW PROPER NUTRITION FUELS YOUR BODY AND MIND

Over 2,000 years ago, Hippocrates, the father of modern medicine, said, 'Let food be thy medicine, and medicine be thy food.'[104] This ancient wisdom still holds true with a growing body of research linking nutrition to mental and physical wellbeing.[105]

Your Brain is Hungry

Your brain is the most energy-demanding organ in your body. Despite making up only 2% of your body weight, it consumes 20% of your energy. Unlike muscles, which store energy for later use, your brain runs on a *constant* fuel supply. And like any high-performance machine, it needs the right fuel to function at its best.

For millennia, humans ate to survive. There was no 'dieting'. Our ancestors weren't concerned with counting macros or meal plans; they ate whatever they could hunt, gather or grow. Calories were scarce, and every meal was a matter of life or death. Their bodies evolved to extract the maximum nutrition from whole, natural foods. Today's nutrient-rich foods support a different kind of resilience: exams, lectures and studying.

Every nutrient-dense meal – leafy greens, lean proteins, nuts, seeds, and healthy fats – provides this. These foods are packed with vitamins, minerals and antioxidants that support cognitive function, improve memory retention and enhance problem-solving abilities.

Key nutrients like omega-3 fatty acids, B vitamins and antioxidants play significant roles in brain health:

- **Omega-3** (fish, walnuts, flaxseeds) strengthens brain cell communication.

- **B vitamins** (eggs, leafy greens, legumes) power neurotransmitter production.

- **Antioxidants** (berries, dark chocolate, nuts) protect your brain from stress.

- **Magnesium** (pumpkin seeds, almonds, spinach) supports stress resilience and energy production.

- **Protein & healthy fats** (lean meats, avocados, nuts) provide slow-releasing energy for sustained focus.

When you fuel an afternoon lecture or study session with crisps and energy drinks, you're more likely to feel drained, irritable and unable to absorb information. Nutrient-dense foods help you stay consistent, focused and resilient.

THE GUT-BRAIN CONNECTION: WHY YOUR DIET AFFECTS YOUR MOOD

Ever felt butterflies in your stomach before a big exam? It's not just nerves; it's a sign of your gut–brain connection. Known as the 'second brain', your gut has its own complex nervous system (the enteric nervous system), which plays a major role in shaping mood, stress response and even immune response.[106]

Think of this connection as a motorway of signals travelling back and forth between the gut and the brain. One of these is the vagus nerve (remember this from the Breathe Pillar?). When your gut is in balance, it sends calming signals to help you manage stress and regulate mood. But if it's out of balance, this communication gets scrambled, contributing to symptoms of anxiety, depression and brain fog.

Your gut microbiome, a community of microorganisms, works 24/7 to support brain function. Nearly 90% of serotonin, the 'feel-good' hormone, is produced in your gut.

In moments of stress, the gut-brain connection kicks into high alert. The sudden urge to use the bathroom before a big presentation or exam is your body going into fight-or-flight mode, prioritising survival and sending signals to clear your system.[107] Processed foods, sugary snacks and unhealthy fats disrupt the balance of bacteria in your gut. This imbalance triggers inflammation, affecting your brain.

If you've heard the term 'psychobiotics', you might know about the link between diet and mental health. Psychobiotic diets are rich in probiotics (live beneficial bacteria) and prebiotics (the food that feeds those bacteria).[108] These support the gut microbiome. A study in 2017 found that people who follow psychobiotic-rich diets reported lower levels of stress and anxiety.[109] Other studies found that fibre-rich diets full of probiotics and anti-inflammatory compounds boost gut health, reduce inflammation and promote a more balanced mental state.[110]

Big life changes, like moving to a new city or starting university (or both), disrupt your gut microbiome. New foods, altered sleep schedules, and increased stress shift the balance of bacteria in your gut. Research indicates that long-term stress leads to changes in gut bacteria and increases intestinal permeability, potentially affecting your mood.[111] But small dietary changes can rebuild resilience from the inside out.

Further research suggests a strong connection between food choices and the body's physiological and emotional responses. The foods we eat are hardwired into the brain's neural circuits, influencing mood and cravings. Certain foods, especially those high in sugar, fat, and salt, activate the brain's reward system, triggering the release of dopamine, the neurotransmitter responsible for pleasure and motivation. When you eat hyper-palatable foods (like sweets, fast food or crisps), your brain rewards you with a surge of dopamine. The more you indulge, the more your brain craves these foods for emotional comfort. Research shows that highly processed foods activate the brain's reward centres in a similar way to addictive substances like tobacco and alcohol. This helps explain why it's easier to binge on crisps than on carrots.

If you're feeling homesick or struggling with university stress, your food habits might be reinforcing those emotions. Ultra-processed foods can cause energy crashes and mood dips, making you feel worse over time.

WHAT YOU EAT MATTERS

In a balanced state, your microbiome (the community of bacteria, fungi, and other microbes) and your virome (the collection of viruses that live in and on you) work together with your immune system to maintain health. They help regulate inflammation, support gut integrity, and ensure your immune system responds appropriately to real threats.

But when your diet is high in ultra-processed foods (UPFs), often loaded with additives, emulsifiers, and artificial sweeteners, it can disrupt this delicate ecosystem.

Some research suggests that certain components in UPFs can trigger an immune response similar to how your body might respond to a pathogen. While the microbiome and virome don't "treat" UPFs like viruses or bacteria, these foods can alter microbial balance, increase gut permeability ("leaky gut"), and promote low-grade, chronic inflammation, much like the body's response to an actual threat. So, in a way, eating UPFs can confuse or overwhelm the immune system, leading it to react as if something dangerous has entered the body.

Have you ever eaten a big, greasy meal and felt tired and sluggish afterwards? That's inflammation at work. This is your body's natural defence mechanism, triggered to protect you from harmful bacteria, viruses and toxins. In the short term (acute phase), inflammation helps your body heal after an injury or infection. When you scrape your knee or catch a cold, it repairs the tissue. However, chronic inflammation – the long-term activation of this immune response – tells a different story. Rather than protecting your body, prolonged inflammation is disruptive, creating consistent 'background noise' that leads to brain fog and mood disturbances, affecting your ability to perform academically and socially.

Imagine trying to study for an exam in the middle of a construction site. The noise and distraction would make it nearly impossible to focus. That's what's happening in your brain when your body is inflamed; it's struggling to function in a chaotic environment.

THE POWER OF MITOCHONDRIA

We've explored the brain and gut, but there's a missing piece of the puzzle: mitochondria. These tiny organelles, often called the 'powerhouses' of your cells, are responsible for converting food into usable energy. This energy fuels everything you do, from staying focused in a lecture to your late-night study session.

But mitochondria aren't just about energy; they're essential for peak brain function. Particularly under pressure, your mitochondria work overtime, helping you stay focused. Supporting your mitochondria through proper nutrition gives you an edge when you need it most.[112]

Mitochondria rely on specific nutrients to produce energy. B vitamins, magnesium, CoQ10 and antioxidants are essential for optimal mitochondrial function:

- **B vitamins** power energy production
- **Magnesium** prevents mental and physical fatigue
- **CoQ10** vital for mitochondrial health
- **Antioxidants** shield mitochondria from damage

A nutrient-rich diet supports mitochondrial efficiency, boosting endurance, concentration and resilience under academic pressure. When your diet lacks essential nutrients, your mitochondria can't function efficiently. You're left drained, mentally foggy and prone to stress. In fact, consuming unhealthy food actively damages your mitochondria. Your food choices don't just fuel your body. They fuel every cell, every thought, every movement.

THE IMMUNE SYSTEM

Your immune system thrives on nutrients like vitamin C, zinc and antioxidants to fight infections and keep inflammation in check. Eating a diet rich in colourful vegetables, lean proteins, and healthy fats keeps your defences strong, helping you stay well under academic pressure.

WHAT YOU EAT DIRECTLY AFFECTS YOUR ACADEMIC PERFORMANCE

Studies show that students who consume high-quality proteins, complex carbohydrates and healthy fats perform better in cognitive tasks and memory retention.

In the next chapter, we'll explore how poor nutrition doesn't just leave you feeling sluggish, it actively sabotages focus, memory and mood. Once you understand what's happening beneath the surface, you'll be ready to fuel your brain for success.

CHAPTER 11:

THE DOUBLE-EDGED SWORD OF CONVENIENCE

'We are living in a world where food has become more about convenience than nourishment.'

Unknown

Ever wonder why that first bite of chocolate cake feels so irresistible? Why, despite your best intentions, it's so difficult to resist another slice of pizza? It isn't about willpower, but deep survival instincts guided by evolution.

Our love for sugar and fat isn't just preference; it's hardwired into our biology. That dopamine hit we get when we eat these foods signals to our brains, 'This is a survival win!' And, for most of history, it was.

Today, we face a unique challenge: foods look good and taste good, while being anything but good. These UPFs are engineered for convenience. They're cheap and easy to get hold of. But the real cost is our physical and mental wellbeing.

At university, convenience and budget drive you towards UPFs as the 'easy option' when you're low on time or funds. Yet, the highly processed, sugar-laden and fat-packed foods dominating your day-to-day are far removed from what our ancestors feasted on.

Modern research links UPFs directly to health risks like diabetes, heart disease and some cancers.[113] And these aren't just long-term risks; they impact your life now.

In this chapter, we'll dive into the world of UPFs, exploring why they're so hard to resist, how the food industry uses powerful marketing strategies to hook us, and the impact of UPFs on our health, the environment and society. By understanding how UPFs shape daily choices, from the 'quick bites' between classes to budget-friendly meal deals, you can begin to make informed decisions that nourish both your mind and body.

THE EVOLUTIONARY DRIVE FOR SUGAR AND FAT

To understand why we crave UPFs, let's travel back in time. Imagine two early humans, Ayak and Eloa, living 14,000 years ago in Mehrgarh (located in Balochistan, Pakistan). One day, Ayak stumbles upon a tree full of sweet fruit. She eats one, feels satisfied, and moves on. The next day, when she returns, the tree is bare. Back then, missing out on food was serious; starvation claimed 15–20% of the population.[114]

Now, meet Eloa. She has a genetic mutation that makes her brain process sugar differently. When she tastes the fruit, her brain floods with dopamine, urging her to eat more. She eats as much as she can, storing up extra calories as fat. The next day, when she finds the tree empty, she has energy reserves to rely on.

Over time, people like Eloa, those with an instinct for 'stocking up' on high-calorie foods, were more likely to survive. Fast-forward millennia, and these cravings still guide us. Back then, they gave us an evolutionary edge. Now, they lead us to reach for snacks when tired or stressed, even if we're not burning through calories like ancient hunters.[115]

Imagine Ayak and Eloa as students today. After a long day of classes, Ayak grabs a burger, feels satisfied, and moves on. Eloa, driven by her genetic craving, orders a burger, fries, Coke and dessert. She's biologically driven to load up on calories, so she eats more and feels stuffed. But the next day, she's back for more.

Our brains, still operating on survival instincts, are wired to consume whenever possible. For most of human history, scarcity shaped our eating habits. But now our brains continue to shout, 'Eat now, because tomorrow it could be gone!', even though food is never far away.

THE RISE OF UPFs

For early humans, people ate what they could hunt, gather or grow. This approach provided a steady diet of nutrient-rich, unprocessed foods. But as cities grew and populations expanded, people began losing the time, space and skills to produce their own food. Further advances in food science introduced refrigeration, canning and preservatives, allowing food to last longer and travel further. Then came mass production. Food became profit, leading to the birth of UPFs.

To meet the demands of urban lifestyles, the food industry prioritises convenience, taste and long shelf life. Fresh goods spoil quickly and require time to prepare, so companies rely on additives, preservatives and processing techniques that keep foods looking and tasting fresh for weeks, months, even years.

However, the food industry understands the human brain. Researchers know the power of dopamine. Neuroscientists and food scientists engineer specific combinations of sugar, fat and salt to maximise cravings, driving demand and increasing consumption.[116] The development of synthetic additives, from sweeteners to flavour enhancers, makes UPFs hyper-palatable, hijacking our senses.

UPFs are cheap, convenient and designed to be addictive. The global food industry is one of the largest and most profitable sectors globally. Companies like Nestlé, Unilever, PepsiCo and Kraft Heinz thrive, maximising profits while minimising nutrition.[117]

What Exactly Are Ultra-Processed Foods?

Before we dive into the impact UPFs have on your health, let's clarify what they are. Ultra-processed foods are industrial formulations that typically contain five or more ingredients, many of which you wouldn't recognise as food in its natural state. These ingredients include artificial additives like preservatives, sweeteners, colourings, emulsifiers and flavour enhancers. Think of packaged snacks, sugary drinks, instant noodles and fast food. If it comes in a package and has a long shelf life, chances are it's ultra-processed food.

A helpful way to identify UPFs is by using the **NOVA food classification system**, developed by researchers to categorise foods based on their level of processing.[118] This system places food into four groups:

1. **Unprocessed or minimally processed foods**: Fresh fruits, vegetables, grains, meat and fish.

2. **Processed culinary ingredients**: Oils, butter, sugar and salt.

3. **Processed foods**: Canned vegetables, cheeses and freshly made bread.

4. **Ultra-processed foods**: Soft drinks, instant soups, crisps, ready meals, bread, cakes and biscuits.

The key difference between processed foods and ultra-processed foods is that UPFs are designed for long shelf lives, convenience and irresistible taste. They are stripped of nutrients and loaded with chemicals to make them hyper-palatable.[119]

The Global Experiment: Overfed but Undernourished

We are living in what some researchers call a 'global experiment.'[120] It's not being conducted in labs, and there aren't scientists in white coats monitoring us, but it's happening. The results are worrying. Unlike traditional experiments, this one is playing out in real time, across entire populations, with billions of people unknowingly participating.

The UK, US and Australia are leading the charge in UPF consumption. This dramatic shift in eating habits has happened incredibly fast, faster than we can fully understand the long-term consequences.

While research already links UPFs to obesity, diabetes, heart disease and mental health issues, the true extent of the impact remains unknown. Some scientists warn that the effects of high UPF consumption may not just be personal but generational, potentially altering gut microbiomes, metabolism and even genetic health for future populations.

The food industry never tested the long-term effects of replacing real food with processed alternatives – yet here we are, the test subjects of a worldwide dietary shift. The question is: will we wait for the full results, or take control of our food choices now?

How much of the food you eat is UPFs? Do you think it's 10%? or even 50%? **It's over 70% for the average UK student.**[121] This is a staggering statistic, highlighting how deeply these foods have infiltrated our lives. A study found that for every 10% increase in UPF consumption, there was a 12% higher risk of developing cancer.[122] Sugar, fats, and salt fill us up. But what about the vitamins, minerals, fibre and antioxidants we need to thrive? Many of us are overfed but undernourished. It's no wonder you are exhausted the moment you open your eyes.

A TYPICAL DAY ON A UPF DIET

Busy days and tight budgets can make a quick meal feel like the obvious solution, but have you ever stopped to think just how much of that 'quick and easy' food is ultra-processed?

Here's a closer look at what a UPF-dominated day might look like and how to swap in some easy gut-friendly alternatives:

Breakfast: You start your day with cereal and a slice of toast. Unless you're making the bread yourself or sticking to whole porridge oats, you're starting your day with a hefty dose of UPFs. And that orange juice? Well, unless it's freshly squeezed, it's been sitting in storage for years before hitting the supermarket shelves.

Try This Instead:

- Overnight oats with frozen berries and a spoon of nut butter
- Boiled eggs & fruit
- Natural yoghurt with seeds and a drizzle of honey

All quick, affordable and packed with real nutrients.

Lunch Grabbing a sandwich, packet of crisps and fizzy drink from the corner shop might seem like the easiest option, but that combo is a UPF bomb. The bread, processed meat, and crisps are full of preservatives, emulsifiers and flavour enhancers.

Try This Instead:

- Wholegrain wrap with hummus, salad and boiled egg or tuna
- Leftover roast veggies & grains tossed into a salad box
- Soup & seeded bread (bonus if you batch cook your own)

Dinner: A microwaveable pasta dish or takeaway pizza might feel like a stress-free win, but the reality is you're eating a plate full of ultra-processed ingredients. The sauce, dough, even the cheese, they're all designed for taste and shelf life, not nutrition.

Try This Instead:

- Stir-fry with frozen veg, egg or tofu and wholegrain noodles
- Baked sweet potato with beans, avocado or cottage cheese

- Wrap pizza, use a wholegrain wrap as your base, add a few spoonfuls of passata or tomato purée, sprinkle with grated cheese, and cook it in a frying pan with a lid until the cheese melts. Add spinach, peppers or any leftovers on top for bonus points.

Snacks: Protein bar? Chocolate bar? Packet of crisps? All dressed up as convenient, but nearly always ultra-processed, with added sugars, sweeteners and artificial flavours.

Try This Instead:

- A handful of nuts & dark chocolate
- An Apple with peanut butter
- Boiled eggs, carrots & hummus
- Popcorn (popped at home with olive oil & sea salt)

You don't need a full kitchen or tons of time, just a few smart swaps that keep you energised, focused and thriving through your day.

FOOD MARKETING

It's not entirely our fault. Food companies are masters at convincing us their products are healthy, even when they're not. Labels like 'low-fat', 'high-protein' or 'organic' leave you thinking you're making a healthy choice.

Even protein bars are marketed as the go-to snack for health-conscious people, but if you flip over the packet, you'll often find a long list of artificial ingredients, refined sugars and preservatives. It's essentially a glorified chocolate bar wrapped up in health branding. And cereals? They shout about being 'wholegrain' or 'low-fat', but many are packed with sugar and artificial flavourings. A brief look at the ingredients list or NOVA classification rating helps you identify what's real vs what's marketing.

HOW TO SPOT A UPF

- Long ingredient lists
- Additives you can't pronounce
- Bright, flashy packaging
- Health claims that sound too good to be true

HOW THE FOOD INDUSTRY USES TOBACCO INDUSTRY TACTICS

Let's go back a few decades. The tobacco industry knew their products were deadly; they caused cancer, heart disease and, ultimately, death. But they hid the truth. By using doctors in their advertisements, insisting they were an aid for health conditions like asthma, and using celebrity endorsements, they promoted smoking.

The food industry is pulling the same tricks. UPFs are engineered to be as addictive as possible. Just like tobacco companies spent decades denying the truth, food companies are downplaying the harm. It's only a matter of time before society realises the damage.

We're all part of this global food experiment, but the good news is that we don't have to be passive participants. Now that you know what UPFs are doing to your health and your world, you can make better choices.

HIDDEN ADDITIVES

Additives are added during manufacturing to enhance flavour, texture, and shelf life. Many have no nutritional value and solely improve the sensory experience of eating. Take emulsifiers, which are used to blend ingredients like oil and water. These are commonly found in products like ice cream, mayonnaise and baked goods. While they make these foods smoother and more stable, certain emulsifiers disrupt the gut microbiome, contributing to inflammation and metabolic disorders like obesity and diabetes.[123]

Artificial sweeteners found in diet drinks and low-calorie snacks are also problematic. While they seem like a healthier alternative, studies suggest that artificial sweeteners disrupt your body's ability to regulate blood sugar and lead to increased cravings for sweet, calorie-dense foods.

UPFS AND THE GUT - BRAIN AXIS

When you eat nutrient-rich whole foods, you support a healthy microbiome, regulating your emotions and mental wellbeing.[124] When your diet is dominated by UPFs, this balance is thrown off.

UPFs contain low amounts of fibre and are high in sugar and unhealthy fats, feeding harmful bacteria in your gut while starving beneficial bacteria. This imbalance leads to gut dysbiosis, a condition where the bad bacteria outnumber the good, causing chronic inflammation and increasing your risk of mental health problems like anxiety and depression.

In fact, research has shown that people who consume a diet high in UPFs are more likely to experience depression than those who eat a diet rich in whole foods.[125] This is because UPFs promote inflammation in both your body, interfering with neurotransmitter production and leading to mood imbalances.

SUGAR IS A PUBLIC HEALTH CRISIS

Sugar is one of the most problematic ingredients in UPFs, and hidden in more places than you might think. From sauces to cereals, sugar exists under different names like dextrose, maltose and agave nectar. This makes it easy to consume far more sugar than you realise, contributing to a range of health problems, from weight gain to diabetes.

One of the biggest issues with sugar is how it affects your brain. Sugar triggers a dopamine release, but it's often followed by an energy crash, leaving you tired, irritable and craving more sugar.

OVEREATING

One of the most insidious effects of UPFs is how they interfere with your body's ability to regulate hunger. When you eat, your body releases hormones like leptin, signalling to your brain that you're full. UPFs disrupt this process, making it harder for your brain to receive these signals.

This disruption is partly due to their high sugar and fat content overstimulating the brain's reward system. It's also due to the lack of fibre in UPFs, as fibre plays a key role in slowing digestion and keeping you full for longer.

As a result, people who consume a diet high in UPFs are more likely to eat larger portions and consume more calories than those who eat a diet rich in whole, unprocessed foods. This leads to weight gain and affects your energy levels, making you lethargic and unmotivated.

Over time, overeating and exhaustion contribute to metabolic disorders like obesity, insulin resistance and heart disease. And because UPFs disrupt your brain's natural hunger signals, breaking free from unhealthy eating habits is difficult.

The bottom line is, you can make more informed choices about what you eat. Armed with this knowledge, you can choose foods that nourish you, moving beyond the empty promises of UPFs. The good news? You don't need to completely overhaul your diet overnight to start seeing results. Even small shifts away from UPFs, like swapping that protein bar for a piece of fruit or whole nuts, can restore energy and focus.

CHAPTER 12:

SMART EATING ON A STUDENT BUDGET

> '*Every time you eat or drink, you are either feeding disease or fighting it.*'
>
> *Heather Morgan*

Imagine waking up feeling clear-headed, focused and energised. Imagine having steady energy throughout the day, instead of crashing mid-afternoon after a sugary snack. The good news? You don't need to eat kale salads or spend a fortune on organic groceries.

This chapter is packed with practical, budget-friendly hacks to fuel your brain, boost your energy, and keep you thriving, without blowing your student loan. Let's dive in!

Hack #1:
STAY HYDRATED – THE SIMPLEST BRAIN BOOST

Why It Works

Your brain is 80% water. Being just 2% dehydrated can slow your thinking, fog your memory and drain your focus, and you might not even realise it's happening.

Coffee, fizzy drinks and energy drinks worsen dehydration, not fix it. The real brain boost? Simple water.

How To Do It

1. Start your day with a glass of water before coffee or tea.
2. Carry a refillable bottle everywhere.
3. Swap fizzy drinks for water, herbal tea or lemon water.

QUICK WIN

Next time you're about to grab a fizzy drink or coffee, pause and drink water first. You'll feel sharper, steadier, and you'll avoid the dreaded sugar crash.

Next Steps Make water your default drink. Train your tastebuds by adding lemon, mint, or cucumber slices if you need a flavour boost.

Research Insight: Well hydrated students perform better on cognitive tests sharper focus, better memory, and faster thinking.[126] Even mild dehydration quietly sabotages your energy and performance. Water is your secret weapon.

Hack #2:
READ FOOD LABELS – OUTSMART SNEAKY MARKETING

Understanding what's in your food is key to making healthier choices. Many products are full of hidden sugars and nasty additives that mess with your energy levels. Learning how to read food labels is an easy way to avoid UPFs.

Remember: Whole foods don't have an ingredients list.

How To Do It

1. If a product has more than five ingredients, it's probably not the best option.

2. Keep an eye out for hidden sugars under names like sucrose, high-fructose corn syrup, dextrose or maltose.

3. Stick to real, whole foods like fruits, vegetables, meat, nuts, seeds and wholegrains.

QUICK WIN

Next time you're at the supermarket, take a couple of extra minutes to read the labels.

Next Steps The simplest trick? Stick to real food. If it doesn't need a label, like fresh fruit, vegetables, eggs, meat, nuts and whole grains, it's likely a better choice.

Research Insight Public Health England links UPF heavy diets to higher rates of depression and chronic inflammation.[127]

Hack #3:
EAT A SAVOURY BREAKFAST – START YOUR DAY STRONG

Why It Works

A high-protein savoury breakfast helps stabilise your energy and keeps you full longer. Eggs, Greek yoghurt, feta and avocado on wholegrain toast, or porridge with nuts and seeds are great brain-fuelling options. Because let's face it, cereal, pastries, toast with jam, or sweetened yoghurts are all filled with sugar and are basically a dessert disguised as breakfast. The problem? These foods spike your blood sugar, making you crash later. In contrast, a protein-rich savoury breakfast provides steady fuel for your brain and body.

The Protein Leverage Hypothesis

Your body craves a certain amount of protein each day. If you don't get enough, you're more likely to overeat calories from fats and carbohydrates in an attempt to compensate. By prioritising protein in your first meal, you can help prevent unnecessary snacking and energy crashes later in the day.

Traditional Diets Have It Right

Around the world, savoury breakfasts are the norm. Many traditional diets prioritise protein and healthy fats in the morning, think miso soup and fish in Japan, beans and eggs in Latin America, or cheese and olives in the Mediterranean. Instead of relying on sugary, processed foods, many cultures simply eat leftovers from dinner, which naturally creates a more balanced, protein-rich first meal of the day. This approach makes meal prep easier, reduces food waste and provides a nutrient-dense start to the morning.

How To Do It

1. Choose eggs, Greek yoghurt, leftover veggies, and tinned fish.
2. Use leftovers, make breakfast easy and cheap.
3. Aim for 20–30g of protein at breakfast to keep hunger in check.

QUICK WIN

Tomorrow, swap your usual breakfast for eggs or Greek yoghurt. See how much better you feel by midday.

Next Steps Plan your breakfasts around a protein source and notice the difference in your hunger and energy levels. Batch-prep breakfast: Boil a few eggs at the start of the week or make a batch of savoury overnight oats with Greek yoghurt, seeds and nuts, so you always have something ready.

Research Insight Students who ate high-protein, low-sugar breakfasts performed better in cognitive tasks than those who opted for high-sugar and low-protein meals.[128]

Hack #4:

EAT THE RAINBOW – MORE COLOUR = MORE NUTRIENTS

Why it Works Your body thrives on variety. The more colours on your plate, the better your nutrient intake. Different colours in fruits and vegetables come from different phytonutrients, health-boosting plant compounds that support your immune system, brain function and energy levels.

How To Do It

1. Red foods (like tomatoes, peppers, and berries) are great for heart health and fighting inflammation.

2. Orange foods (like carrots, sweet potatoes, and pumpkin) are packed with beta-carotene, which is amazing for your eyesight.

3. Green foods (like spinach, broccoli, kale) are full of fibre and help with digestion.

4. Blue & purple foods (blueberries, aubergine, grapes) are loaded with antioxidants for brain health.

QUICK WIN

Include at least three different coloured veggies in your next meal.

Next Steps Challenge yourself to eat as many different colours as possible throughout the week.

Research Insight People who eat a diverse, colourful diet have sharper cognitive function, stronger immune systems and better overall health.[129]

Hack #5:
PSYCHOBIOTIC DIET - BOOST YOUR MOOD AND BRAIN HEALTH THROUGH YOUR GUT

Why It Works

Your gut makes 90% of your serotonin - the 'feel-good' hormone that regulates mood, sleep and memory. It's also home to trillions of bacteria, forming a complex ecosystem known as your gut microbiome. This microbiome doesn't just influence digestion – it directly impacts your brain, emotions and stress resilience.

The **psychobiotic diet** focuses on nourishing your gut by eating foods rich in:

- **Fibre.** The fuel that feeds beneficial bacteria
- **Probiotics.** Live 'good' bacteria that support gut health
- **Prebiotics.** Plant fibres that act as food for the good bacteria

By supporting a healthy gut, you boost mental clarity, resilience and emotional wellbeing, vital for academic success.

How To Do It

1. Eat more fermented foods like yoghurt, kefir, sauerkraut and miso
2. Increase your fibre intake with fruits, vegetables, whole grains and legumes
3. Include a variety of plant-based foods to ensure diversity.

QUICK WIN

Try adding one fermented food to your diet this week. Start with a small serving of yoghurt, sauerkraut or miso soup. Your gut and your brain will thank you.

Next Steps

1. Consistently expand the variety of fermented and prebiotic-rich foods in your daily routine.

2. Incorporate different fermented foods like kimchi, kombucha and tempeh.

3. Increase your intake of prebiotic foods, such as garlic, onions and oats.

Tip: Keep track of how these foods make you feel by using a journal to tailor your diet for optimal gut and brain health.

Research Insight A diet rich in probiotics and prebiotics significantly reduces anxiety, enhances cognitive function and improves stress resilience.[130]

Hack #6:
FIRST – A SIMPLE HABIT TO STABILISE ENERGY AND FOCUS

Why It Works Starting your meal with vegetables is a game-changer for your blood sugar, energy and mental clarity. Vegetables are packed with fibre, which slows the absorption of sugar into your bloodstream. This helps stabilise your energy throughout the day, reduces insulin spikes, and supports better digestion.

This approach, known as food sequencing, significantly lowers post-meal blood sugar compared to eating carbohydrates first. Many cultures naturally follow this habit – think of Italian antipasti or Middle Eastern mezze, where meals begin with vegetable-based starters.

How To Do It

1. Always eat your veggies first, before diving into carbs or protein.
2. Include a simple starter: a handful of salad, sliced cucumbers, or a few cooked greens before your main meal.

QUICK WIN

At your next meal, eat the veggies on your plate first. Before moving on to the carbs or protein. Notice how much more stable your energy feels afterwards!

Next Steps Make "veggies first" your everyday habit, no matter the meal. Over time, you'll experience better digestion, fewer energy crashes, and sharper focus.

Research Insight Eating vegetables and protein before carbohydrates reduces post-meal blood glucose spikes by up to 29%. Even small shifts in meal order create powerful benefits for your health and mental performance[131].

Hack #7:
MINDFUL EATING - TUNE IN BEFORE YOU DIVE IN

Why it Works

We've all done it, eating while scrolling through social media or watching Netflix. However, mindless eating leads to overeating and messes with your digestion. Being mindful about what and why you're eating helps you make better choices and prevent stress-related overeating.

How To Do It

1. Ask yourself if you're hungry, stressed, bored or seeking comfort.

2. Avoid eating in front of a screen.

3. Chew slowly and put your fork down between bites.

QUICK WIN

Next time you're about to snack, pause and ask yourself if you're really hungry. Have a glass of water first. Sometimes we confuse hunger with thirst.

Next Steps Commit to mindful eating for just one meal a day, no distractions, just focusing on your food. You'll start reconnecting with your natural hunger and fullness signals.

Research Insight University students who practised mindful eating reported lower emotional eating scores, reduced anxiety, and better awareness of hunger cues.[132]

Hack #8:
ADD APPLE CIDER VINEGAR - A SIMPLE BLOOD SUGAR SECRET

Drinking a small amount of apple cider vinegar (ACV) before your largest meal of the day can stabilise your blood sugar by slowing down the absorption of carbohydrates, keeping your energy levels more balanced. In addition to regulating blood sugar, ACV supports healthy digestion, making it a simple yet effective way to enhance both your physical and mental wellbeing. Incorporating this practice, alongside starting meals with vegetables, creates a powerful combination to help you thrive.

How to Use Apple Cider Vinegar:

1. Mix 1 tablespoon of ACV in a glass of water (use a straw to protect your teeth).

2. Drink it before your largest meal to prevent blood sugar spikes and crashes.

QUICK WIN

Before your next large meal, add a splash of ACV to a glass of water.

Next Steps Incorporate this vinegar hack before any carb-heavy meals.

Research Insight A study from Diabetes UK found that ACV significantly reduced blood sugar spikes after meals and supported digestive health.[133]

Hack #9:
TIME-RESTRICTED EATING – GIVE YOUR BODY TIME TO REST

With food available 24/7, it's easy to fall into the habit of snacking all day (and night). But constant grazing can stress your digestive system, impact sleep, and leave you feeling sluggish.

Time-restricted eating (TRE) is a simple approach that encourages you to eat within a set window during the day, giving your body time to reset, repair and realign with its natural rhythms.

Why It Works

Giving your body a break from digestion boosts your metabolism, supports gut health, balances blood sugar, and allows vital repair processes to kick in, like autophagy, where your body clears out damaged cells and toxins.

How To Do It

1. Stick to 2–3 solid meals a day and try to avoid constant snacking.

2. Aim to finish eating 2–3 hours before bed – this gives your digestive system time to wind down, improving sleep and next-day energy.

3. If your schedule allows, keep your eating window to around 10–12 hours (e.g. 8 a.m. to 6/8 p.m.), but don't stress about perfection. Flexibility matters.

QUICK WIN

Tonight, simply stop eating 3 hours before bed. You'll likely sleep better and wake up feeling clearer and lighter.

Next Steps Once you've built the habit of eating at regular times and avoiding late-night snacks, you can experiment with a slightly shorter eating window or earlier dinners for even more benefits, including better focus and digestion.

Research Insight Studies show that even gentle time-restricted eating patterns can improve metabolic health, support energy levels, and reduce inflammation, all without strict calorie counting or extreme fasting.[134]

Hack #10:

PLAN YOUR MEALS - SAVE TIME, MONEY AND BOOST YOUR NUTRITION

Meal planning isn't just for fitness influencers; it's one of the easiest ways to stick to a healthy diet on a budget. It helps you avoid last-minute junk food runs while saving money and ensuring you're fuelling your body.

How To Do It

1. Pick five simple meals that take 15 minutes or less to prepare (stir-fries, salads or pasta with veggies).

2. Buy in bulk (frozen and tinned veggies and fruits are much cheaper).

3. Prep your meals or ingredients in advance.

QUICK WIN

Pick one day this week to plan your meals. You don't need to go overboard choose your meals, buy what you need and prep the ingredients.

Next Steps Incorporate meal planning into your weekly routine. It doesn't need to be complicated, but planning ahead will save you time, money and stress when it comes to eating well.

Research Insight

Studies show that students who regularly plan their meals are more likely to have a healthier diet, have a lower risk of obesity, and save money compared to those who don't meal plan. Planning ahead increases the likelihood of making balanced, nutritious food choices and helps reduce impulsive eating, which is often less healthy and more expensive[135].

Eating Healthy on a Budget

1. Prioritise Nutrient-Dense Foods

- Frozen vegetables and fruits
- Whole grains (brown rice, quinoa, whole-grain bread)
- Legumes (lentils, chickpeas, black beans)
- Eggs, which are an inexpensive source of protein
- Canned fish (like tuna or salmon in water)

2. Cook at Home

- Avoid eating out frequently.
- Prepare large batches of food and freeze portions.

3. Reduce Food Waste

- Use leftovers for soups or pasta toppings.
- Store food properly to prevent spoilage.

4. Student Discounts

- Some grocery stores offer student discounts; bring your ID when shopping.
- Explore campus food resources, like food pantries or subsidised meal plans.

5. Kitchen Tools

A slow cooker or Instant Pot can help make cooking easy, budget-friendly and energy-efficient. Running a slow cooker for eight hours costs about the same as keeping a light bulb on, making it one of the most cost-effective ways to cook. Plus, it allows you to prepare nutritious home-cooked meals with minimal effort, saving both time and money.

TAKE CONTROL TODAY

Start small: Replace one ultra-processed snack with a whole food option

Budget tip: Look for whole foods on sale or in bulk (oats, vegetables and fruit).

Mindful choice: The next time you're tempted by a quick snack, ask: 'Is this truly nourishing me or just keeping me satisfied for now?' This check-in makes a big difference in helping you choose foods that fuel your body and mind for the long term.

FUEL YOUR BODY, FUEL YOUR MIND

These hacks, from staying hydrated and eating veggies first to trying time-restricted eating, are designed to help you make better choices without breaking the bank. Nourishing your body with the right foods isn't just about feeling good, it's about performing at your best academically, socially and personally. By integrating small changes into your routine, you'll be fuelling your body and mind for long-term success, so you can power through university and beyond. **Start with one small change today**.

PILLAR 5:

CONNECT

FOSTER MEANINGFUL RELATIONSHIPS

FOR WELLBEING

CHAPTER 13:
THE ROLE OF SOCIAL CONNECTIONS

'You can't stay in your corner of the Forest waiting for others to come to you. You have to go to them sometimes.'

A.A. Milne, Winnie-the-Pooh

You've just nailed a presentation, but your heart is still racing, and adrenaline is coursing through your veins. The pressure, the build-up, the sheer focus, it's all still buzzing in your mind. As you step out of the hall, you spot a familiar face, a close friend, waiting for you. They smile and ask, 'How did it go?' You start to recount the experience, their enthusiasm drawing out your excitement. They laugh at your jokes, celebrate your success, and suggest grabbing a coffee to mark the moment. Slowly, the tension eases. It's not just the achievement that brings relief; it's the act of sharing it with someone who truly gets you. This is the power of social connections: they don't just amplify joy; they also help you process the highs and lows of life.

The Science of Connection

Have you ever noticed how being around the right people makes you feel lighter and calmer? It's not just in your head. Your body is biologically wired to thrive on connection. Let's see how.

When someone cheers you on, listens to you or makes you feel seen, your brain releases oxytocin (the 'bonding hormone'). It's your body's social glue, strengthening emotional bonds, reducing stress and promoting physical healing.[136]

People who experience social support during stressful situations tend to have higher oxytocin levels and lower cortisol levels compared to those who feel isolated.[137] Oxytocin calms your stress response, protects your heart and strengthens your immune system.

WHY WE'RE WIRED FOR RELATIONSHIPS

So, why do friendships matter so much? Why does the presence of people you trust make your heart rate slow, your shoulders relax, and your mind a little lighter?

The answer lies in the story of our ancestors. Picture early humans navigating a harsh and unpredictable world. The landscape was rife with dangers: predators, scarce food supplies, and the threat of injury or illness. In such an environment, being alone was tantamount to vulnerability. But together, in a group, humans found safety, strength and the power to thrive.

To ensure humans sought and maintained these bonds, evolution created a reward system for social interaction. When early humans spent time with their tribes, their brains released a cocktail of chemicals: oxytocin for bonding, dopamine for pleasure, and endorphins for comfort. Feel-good hormones reinforced their behaviour.

MODERN TRIBES AND DIGITAL REALITIES

Think of your tribe today. It might be a WhatsApp group lighting up with jokes and memes, a group of friends rallying for a late-night takeaway, or classmates working together on a challenging project. The format has evolved, but the essence remains the same: connection helps us navigate the uncertainties of modern life.

While we may no longer need tribes to fend off predators, we do need them to manage the emotional and mental challenges of today's world. From the stress of exams to the loneliness of living away from home, connection acts as a buffer, reminding us that we're not alone.

THE VAGUS NERVE: YOUR PATHWAY TO CALM AND CONNECTION

Every time you smile, laugh, or have a meaningful conversation, your vagus nerve gets a workout. That's a very good thing. By experiencing meaningful connections, this nerve activates, telling your body to relax, lowering your heart rate, reducing stress and promoting a sense of calm. People with high vagal tone are better at recovering emotionally after challenging events. Social interaction strengthens the vagus nerve, which plays a key role in boosting both mental and physical wellbeing.

ENDORPHINS: THE SOCIAL HIGH

When a friend makes you laugh, your body releases endorphins (natural painkillers and mood boosters). Laughing together increases pain tolerance and strengthens social bonds.[138] So, the next time you find yourself giggling uncontrollably during a late-night study session, remember it's not just fun, it's biology.

WHY CONNECTION IS THE BEST MEDICINE FOR YOUR HEALTH

University stress is inevitable. Deadlines. Exams. Flatmates. Research shows that people with close social ties have stronger immune systems and enjoy better overall health than those who are isolated.[139] This is where friends come in. Having someone to talk to lowers cortisol levels, helping your body remain calm under pressure. This phenomenon, called 'social buffering', is like emotional bubble wrap.

A Supported Heart is a Healthy Heart

Chronic stress is one of the biggest threats to your heart. It leads to high blood pressure, inflammation and an increased risk of heart disease.

However, strong social connections act as a protective shield for your cardiovascular system. Connection isn't just emotionally fulfilling, it's life-saving. People with close social ties are 50% less likely to develop heart disease compared to those who are socially isolated.[140]

Better Sleep and Recovery

Getting quality sleep is like hitting the 'refresh' button for your body and mind. And guess what? Your social connections are the secret ingredient for better sleep. Those with close companions experience fewer sleep disruptions and enjoy deeper, more restorative rest due to regulated cortisol.

Adding Years to Your Life

Strong social ties don't just improve your quality of life; they actively extend it. People with close relationships are 50% more likely to live longer than those who are socially isolated.[141] Loneliness is associated with a 40% increased risk of dementia, while meaningful social ties significantly reduce this risk.[142] Students with larger social networks produce more antibodies than their peers with fewer connections.[143]

Natural Pain Relief

Have you ever noticed how pain seems less intense when you're with someone who cares about you? That's because social connection acts as a natural painkiller.

When you're around friends, your body releases endorphins. Even something as simple as holding a friend's hand during a difficult moment provides relief. This effect isn't just emotional; it's biological.

Whether it's a headache from too much screen time or soreness after a workout, being with others can ease the discomfort. Laughter, conversation and physical touch stimulate oxytocin , lower cortisol, and help your body relax and recover. Distraction also plays a role:

when you're engaged with someone, you're less likely to dwell on the discomfort. So, the next time you're sore after exercise, a good chat or a shared laugh might just help you bounce back faster.

NEUROPLASTICITY: BUILDING A RESILIENT BRAIN

Your brain's ability to change and adapt (neuroplasticity) is the foundation of learning and growth. And guess what? Social interaction is one of the best ways to stimulate it.

Why It Works:

- Engaging in conversations, solving problems with others, and navigating social dynamics create neural pathways in your brain.

- Positive relationships boost levels of BDNF, a protein essential for neuroplasticity.

- Social support aids stress recovery, preserving its ability to adapt.

Students with strong social networks performed better on problem-solving tasks, thanks to enhanced brain plasticity.[144]

FRIENDSHIPS AFFECT OTHERS

One of the most inspiring aspects of connection is how its benefits ripple outwards. When you thrive, you inspire those around you to thrive, too. Happy, healthy individuals influence their friends to adopt better habits, creating a chain reaction of positivity.

Think about it: when your flatmate starts jogging every morning, you're more likely to join in. When your friend swaps junk food for healthier snacks, it inspires you to do the same. Your positivity and healthy habits instil a chain reaction, influencing everyone in your circle to lead better lives. Together, you're building a healthier, happier community.

YOU ARE THE SUM OF FIVE PEOPLE

There's a famous idea that you are the average of the five people you spend the most time with.[145] While it's not a hard rule, they are like your personal Wi-Fi network: boosting your signal or slowing you down. Surround yourself with people whose energy lifts you – those who inspire you to tackle assignments. Join a gym session or laugh when you need it most. Over time, positive attitudes boost positivity.

This doesn't mean cutting ties with friends who are struggling. Supporting and being supported is the core of any meaningful relationship. However, it does mean being intentional about who you allow into your inner circle. If someone consistently brings you down or encourages self-destructive habits, it's worth reflecting on whether that relationship is helping or hindering your growth. At the same time, consider the friend you are to others. Are you uplifting, encouraging and supportive? Or do you bring negativity into the mix? Relationships are reciprocal. When you strive to be a positive influence, you'll naturally attract others who do the same.

BEYOND PEOPLE: THE ROLE OF NATURE

Connection isn't limited to relationships with people. Our bond with the natural world is equally important. This connection, though quieter and less obvious, offers solace in the midst of life's chaos. Fresh air, rustling leaves, sunlight filtering through trees... each of these makes the world a little less overwhelming.[146]

Spending as little as 20 minutes in a natural environment significantly reduces cortisol. Exposure to natural light, fresh air and the gentle rhythm of nature calms the nervous system, restoring a sense of balance and focus.

Shinrin-Yoku: Japan's Prescription for Wellbeing

In Japan, they've taken this understanding of nature's healing power to the next level with shinrin-yoku, or 'forest bathing'. This isn't about hiking or physical exertion; it's about immersing yourself in the sensory experience of the forest.

Imagine standing in a quiet woodland, breathing in the earthy scent of moss and pine, feeling the texture of rough bark under your fingers, and listening to the rustle of wind combing the leaves. It's a full-body experience, designed to quieten your mind and rejuvenate your spirit.

Shinrin-Yoku is not only a cultural tradition but also a science-backed practice. Participants who practise forest bathing experience:

- 16% lower cortisol levels, reducing stress
- Improved mood and energy
- Immunity via phytoncides (antimicrobial compounds released by trees)

There's no need for equipment, strict schedules or goals when outside. It's about being present and engaging all five senses:

- Smell the fresh scent of the forest
- Listen to the birdsong
- Touch the rough bark
- See the shifting light
- Taste the freshness in the air

A Global Lesson from Japan

In the UK, 'green prescriptions' are growing more common. These initiatives encourage individuals to spend time in parks, community gardens or nature reserves. British healthcare now recognises that nature isn't just a luxury, it's essential for physical and mental health.

Social Prescribing: Connecting Through Nature

Building on this idea, social prescribing has emerged as a powerful tool in modern healthcare. Rather than prescribing pills, healthcare professionals now recommend nature-based activities like gardening clubs, conservation groups or outdoor exercise. **It has been shown to be twice as effective as taking chemical antidepressants.**

Social prescribing taps into a basic truth: connection to nature, people or purpose has profound benefits:

- Gentle movement in fresh air boosts physical health.
- Sensory engagement reduces stress and calms the mind.
- Social interaction combats isolation, fostering a sense of belonging.

These programmes are particularly effective for individuals struggling with stress, anxiety or loneliness.

Have you ever noticed how much easier it is to open up to someone when you're walking side by side, rather than sitting across a table from them? Nature has a unique way of breaking down barriers and fostering connection.

You and a friend take a break from the library and walk through a nearby park. At first, you talk about how tough the lecture was and how tired you feel. But as the rhythm of your steps matches each other, you find yourself sharing something deeper. The combination of fresh air, birdsong and the steady pace creates the perfect setting for a genuine conversation.

Time spent in natural settings encourages cooperation, reduces tension and fosters a sense of shared purpose.[147] A study published in *Environment and Behaviour* found that exposure to nature increases prosocial behaviours, decreases antisocial behaviours, and enhances feelings of social connection and satisfaction.

Next time you feel stressed or disconnected, invite someone for a walk. Leave your phone in your pocket, tune into the sounds around you, and see how the conversation flows. You might be surprised at how much easier it feels to connect.

For most of human history, we lived outdoors. Fields, forests and rivers weren't just backdrops; they were life itself. Nature fed, sheltered and healed us. But in the blink of an evolutionary eye, we moved indoors. Now, nearly all of us spend our lives under artificial lights, surrounded by walls.

This sudden shift is unnatural. We're wired to seek out the sights, sounds and smells of the natural world. That's why just stepping outside feels like hitting 'reset' on your brain. Think about it: when was the last time you sat under a tree, walked by water or stood in the sun? These moments remind us of our place in the world. We are not isolated individuals but part of something much bigger.

Even if you can't escape to a forest, small touches of nature make a difference. Open a window. Sit by a sunny spot in your flat. Tend to a houseplant. Each moment reconnects you to a primal bond that restores balance and clarity.

Biophilic Design: Bringing Nature Indoors

Most of us spend 90% of our time indoors, with 65% of that time in our own homes. For a three-year university course, that's two years!

Yet, we can bring nature to us through biophilic design (an approach to creating spaces that mimic the natural world).

Studies have shown the profound effects of biophilic design:

- Desks near windows with a view increase productivity by 25%.
- Adding plants to workspaces boosts productivity by 15%.
- Biophilic design helps students learn 20% faster.
- Hospital patients recover faster (and require less medication) with a view of green spaces.

Connection is Your Greatest Resource

Social connection is a powerful force for health and resilience. It shapes every aspect of wellbeing, from physical health and cognitive performance to emotional stability and stress management. By nurturing relationships with people and nature, you create a support system that allows you to thrive.

CHAPTER 14:
SOCIAL ISOLATION AND LONELINESS

'If you want to go fast, go alone. If you want to go far, go together.'

African Proverb

Imagine a condition affecting the health of millions worldwide that's as damaging as smoking 15 cigarettes a day. It's not a virus or a chronic illness. Yet, its consequences increase the risks of heart disease, depression and even early death. This silent epidemic is loneliness.

Did you know that nearly 92% of students in the UK report feeling lonely?[148] More than 1 in 6 students don't have any friends.[149] Loneliness is an invisible epidemic, a paradox of being constantly connected yet feeling profoundly disconnected. At university, it's easy to assume everyone else is thriving while you're the only one struggling. The truth? Most students experience moments of isolation, even in the busiest lecture halls.

In this chapter, we'll explore why loneliness is so damaging. By examining its evolutionary roots, modern causes and long-term impact, we can understand why it's not just an individual challenge but a systemic issue.

THE LONELINESS GENERATION: WHY DIGITAL CONNECTION ISN'T ENOUGH

Generation Z (born between 1997 and 2010) are statistically the loneliest generation in history, despite unprecedented access to social platforms and communication tools. Generation Alpha (born between 2010 and 2024) are predicted to experience even greater disconnection as technology and social media become more entrenched in daily life.

Why does this happen? Social media offers the illusion of connection. Curated reels highlight the best bits, brunches, parties, and holidays, while hiding struggles and awkward moments. It's a performance, not a reality.

SOCIAL MEDIA AND THE ILLUSION OF SAFETY

And let's face it, texting and social media feel safer than a phone call or an in-person chat. You can take your time, check for mistakes and perfect your words before hitting send. You're not alone in this. Research by psychologist Jean Twenge shows that many young people prefer texting or messaging over speaking face-to-face because it feels less vulnerable.

But the more we rely on controlled, edited interactions, the less we experience spontaneity and authenticity, which builds true connections. Despite 1,000 Instagram followers, how many truly know you? How many could you call at 2 a.m. when you need someone to talk to?

EVOLUTIONARY ROOTS: WHY WE NEED TRIBES

Loneliness isn't just an emotion; it's an evolutionary alarm system. Imagine being alone 30,000 years ago. You'd face predators, starvation and exposure to harsh elements. Your community was your lifeline, offering safety, resources and companionship.

Loneliness affects us psychologically and biologically for a reason. When you feel it, your brain floods your system with cortisol to push you back towards social bonds. In the past, loneliness was useful – it forced humans to seek out their tribe. But in today's world? It's easier to isolate. In a world dominated by social media and convenience-driven routines, finding meaningful connections is harder than ever.

The result? Chronic stress, anxiety and declining mental health. Loneliness can be dangerous.

THE PSYCHOLOGICAL AND PHYSICAL COST OF LONELINESS

- **Increases stress & anxiety**: Loneliness raises cortisol levels, making you feel more anxious, more fatigued, and more emotionally drained.

- **Lowers your immune system**: Chronic loneliness weakens your body's defences, leaving you more vulnerable to illness.

- **Harms your heart**: A study in the American Journal of Cardiology found that loneliness increases the risk of heart disease by 50%.

- **Contributes to cognitive decline**: A 2021 study found that loneliness increases the risk of dementia by 40%.

Simply put, loneliness makes you sicker, more stressed and less able to focus.

WHY SOCIAL MEDIA FEELS GOOD BUT LEAVES YOU EMPTY

Let's face it: social media is addictive, and it's not accidental. One-third of the global population is on Facebook (Meta). Three billion people, billions of hours scrolling. No other company in history has achieved anything like this. But what's behind Facebook's enormous success? Our desire to talk about ourselves.

Every time you post a photo or share a status update, your brain's reward system kicks in. The nucleus accumbens, a part of the brain associated with pleasure, lights up. It's the same for food, sex and socialising. Why does this happen? It's because sharing ourselves strengthens social ties and improves cooperation. Talking about yourself lets you see how others react, allowing you to tweak your behaviour to fit in better.

Robin Dunbar, an anthropologist, proposed that humans can maintain about 150 meaningful relationships, which is known as 'Dunbar's number'. It reflects the capacity of our brains to manage social ties effectively.[150]

Technology has shattered Dunbar's number. Your brain craves intimacy, trust and shared experiences, but when those bonds are missing, your brain sounds the alarm, leaving you feeling lonely, even in a crowd.

THE EVOLUTIONARY COST OF CONVENIENCE

Our ancestors worked hard to maintain their tribes. Hunting, gathering and protecting the group required constant collaboration and communication. And these efforts were rewarded with deep, meaningful relationships. Today, convenience has replaced connection. You can order food to your door, stream lectures from your bed, and scroll through social media instead of meeting up with friends.

But the less effort you put into building relationships, the more isolated you become. And while technology promises to fill the gap, it actually deepens it. Our brains crave the warmth of shared moments and the belonging that once defined human life. Yet today, many of us live isolated lives, disconnected from the communal bonds that once sustained us.

WHY LONLINESS FEELS LIKE REJECTION

One of the most painful aspects of loneliness is that it feels personal. When you're excluded from a group chat, ignored in a lecture, or left out of plans, it stings. This pain is evolutionary. In the past, rejection from the tribe meant death. To avoid this, our brains evolved to treat exclusion as a serious threat, triggering anxiety, sadness and physical pain.

In today's world, social rejection is often subtle and indirect. Yet, the more isolated you feel, the harder it becomes to reach out and reconnect, creating a vicious cycle of loneliness.

Stigma of Loneliness

One of the hardest parts about loneliness is the stigma attached to admitting you're lonely. It makes you feel like you're a failure as a person. At university, where it often seems like everyone else is thriving socially, this feels more intense.

Truthfully, most people feel lonely at some point, especially during transitional periods like starting university. You're not alone; you're just not hearing others talk about it. Loneliness thrives in silence, but breaking free is the first step toward connection.

THE ROLE OF YOUR ENVIRONMENT

Your living environment can either help combat loneliness or make it worse. Single-occupancy studio flats, while convenient, can lead to isolation if efforts aren't made to stay socially connected. Without shared spaces like common rooms or kitchens, opportunities for organic interactions naturally dwindle. This means students in studios need to be more intentional about meeting others, whether that's joining clubs, attending social events, or simply reaching out to neighbours.

HOW TO BUILD CONNECTIONS

1. **Campus Activities**
   - Join clubs, societies or sports teams.
   - Attend campus events like mixers, workshops or fairs.
   - Volunteer for campus initiatives.

2. **Neighbours**
   - Knock on doors or leave a friendly note to say hello.
   - Share casual greetings in hallways or communal areas.
   - Organise a small get-together or invite them for coffee.

3. **Technology**
   - Join campus social media groups or forums.
   - Use apps like Meetup or Bumble BFF to find local friends.
   - Stay connected with classmates through group chats.

4. **Events**
   - Plan casual movie nights, game nights or bring and share meals.
   - Participate in floor or building-wide parties.
   - Go out with peers for meals or explore local attractions.

5. **Shared Interests**
   - Find common hobbies like fitness, music or art.

- Visit local gyms, libraries or cafes.
- Collaborate on projects or study sessions.

6. **Seek Support**
   - Reach out to your Resident Assistant for guidance.
   - Use counselling or mentorship programmes.
   - Share concerns with trusted friends or university staff.

LONLINESS IS NOT A LIFE SENTENCE

Loneliness isn't a failure; it's a call to action. By taking small, intentional steps, you can rewrite the story of disconnection and build the meaningful relationships your mind and body crave.

CHAPTER 15:

FOSTERING A SENSE OF BELONGING

> '*Connection is a practice, not a one-time fix. The more you invest in your relationships, both with people and with nature, the richer your life will become. Start small. Take one action today. Because a life filled with meaningful connection isn't just possible, it's your natural state.*'
>
> *Radha Agrawal*

Loneliness isn't a sign that something is wrong with you; it's a sign that you're human. Just like hunger tells you to eat, loneliness is your brain's way of saying, *'You need connection.'*

Yet, in today's world, where we're constantly plugged in, scrolling and surrounded by digital interactions, real connection feels harder to find than ever. If you're feeling isolated right now, know this: you're not alone, and you're not broken. You are human. Loneliness is a universal experience, especially in a world that's more connected online but increasingly disconnected in reality.

The good news? Loneliness isn't permanent. It's your mind's gentle nudge to reach out, to reconnect, to find your people. And you can. In this chapter, I explore science-backed ways to build belonging, create meaningful relationships and cultivate the deep connections that help you thrive.

THE POWER OF INCLUSIVE COMMUNITIES

University brings together a diverse group of people, creating a unique environment that fosters inclusive communities. An inclusive community isn't just a social group; it's a support network, a source of motivation, and a foundation for shared experiences. Feeling like you belong provides both immediate and long-term health benefits.

Individuals who feel included and accepted are less likely to experience depression and anxiety. This is because inclusive communities create safe spaces for people to share their experiences, struggles and triumphs. Being part of a group also encourages healthier behaviours, as you're more likely to join others in activities like sports, study groups or regular social meetups, all of which boost physical health and combat loneliness.

Building an Inclusive Community: Starting Small

Creating a sense of community doesn't mean joining large organisations or attending every social event. Start with people in your immediate environment, flatmates, course-mates or even familiar faces in the library. Simple gestures, like inviting someone for coffee or organising a group study session, can lead to meaningful connections that grow over time.

Even brief social interactions trigger the release of dopamine, the feel-good neurotransmitter that enhances mood and energy. These micro-interactions require very little time but can significantly impact your overall wellbeing.

PRACTICAL STRATEGIES FOR FOSTERING CONNECTION

Ready to start building your tribe? Let's dive into simple, research-backed hacks you can start today.

Hack #1:
START SMALL – THE 2-MINUTE CONNECTION

Why It Works Loneliness feels overwhelming because we assume connection requires a huge effort. But the reality? Relationships start with tiny moments. A smile. A hello. A simple question.

How To Do It

The 2-Minute Rule: Every day, make a small effort to connect.

- Say hi to someone in class.
- Ask a flatmate how their day is going.
- Send a quick message to check in with a friend.

QUICK WIN FOR SUCCESS

Tomorrow, greet someone new, a classmate, a barista, someone at the bus stop.

Next Steps Build on these interactions. Start with small talk, then progress to sharing thoughts or feelings to deepen the connection.

Research Insight Even brief social interactions like chatting with a classmate, barista, or a stranger, can significantly increase feelings of belonging, happiness and wellbeing. Small moments of connection help combat loneliness and reinforce a sense of social support[151].

Hack #2:
CULTIVATE COMMUNITY – SURROUND YOURSELF WITH ENERGY THAT LIFTS YOU

Why It Works The people you surround yourself with impact on your mood, habits and health. Research shows that the people you spend the most time with influence everything from what you eat, how much you exercise and how much you sleep. So, it's time to get intentional about who's in your inner circle.

How To Do It

1. **Identify your core people:** Spend a few minutes reflecting on the five people you spend the most time with. Are they lifting you up or bringing you down?

2. **Join or start groups:** Whether it's a club, sports team or study group, like-minded individuals strengthen your sense of belonging.

3. **Be proactive:** Reach out by inviting a friend for coffee or joining a local group.

QUICK WIN

This week, invite one person for a coffee.

Next Steps Turn socialising into a habit. Schedule regular catch-ups with friends, whether it's a weekly coffee or a monthly movie night. Make the time to nurture relationships, even when uni life gets hectic.

Research Insight The Harvard Study of Adult Development, one of the longest-running studies in history, found that individuals with strong, supportive relationships were healthier, lived longer, and exhibited better brain function. The quality of your relationships influences your health as much as diet and exercise[152].

Hack #3:
HOUSEPLANTS – BRING CALM AND LIFE INTO YOUR SPACE

Why It Works Add houseplants to your living space. They calm your environment and help connect you with nature, even when you're stuck studying.

How To Do It

1. Start with low-maintenance plants like succulents, spider plants or herbs.

2. Place them where you spend the most time, your desk, near your bed or common areas.

3. Take a few minutes each day to look after them and enjoy doing so.

QUICK WIN

Buy one small plant for your room or workspace. You'll be amazed at how much a little greenery can brighten your mood.

Next Steps Grow your green space by adding more plants over time. Build a small indoor garden or even a windowsill herb collection.

Research Insight Studies show that having plants in your environment can boost focus, lower stress hormones, and promote a sense of calm, all of which support cognitive and emotional wellbeing[153].

FOSTERING A SENSE OF BELONGING

Hack #4:
FACE-TO-FACE TIME – STRENGTHEN YOUR BONDS BEYOND THE SCREEN

Why it Works Social media might keep you in the loop, but it's no substitute for real human interaction. Spending quality in-person time with those you care about boosts your mental health and deepens your connections.

How To Do It

1. Schedule regular meet-ups: A study session or casual catch-up.

2. Turn off notifications: Put your phone away to fully engage in conversations.

3. Choose activities that foster connection: Go for a walk, cook a meal, or hang out.

QUICK WIN

This week, swap one social media scroll for a face-to-face catch-up with a friend, start with a 15-minute coffee break chat and see where it takes you.

Next Steps Make in-person hangouts a regular part of your week. Prioritise them as essential to your wellbeing, not optional extras.

Research Insight People who prioritise face-to-face interactions tend to feel less lonely and report greater life satisfaction than those who primarily connect through social media[154].

Hack #5:

THE 'CONVERSATION DEEPENER' TECHNIQUE – GO BEYOND SMALL TALK TO BUILD REAL BONDS

Why It Works: Many social interactions remain on autopilot, quick greetings, generic check-ins, and surface-level chat. But when you ask more thoughtful, open-ended questions, you spark an authentic connection. Deeper conversations help build trust, strengthen relationships, and create a genuine sense of belonging.

How To Do It

1. Instead of 'How are you?' try 'What's something good that happened to you this week?'

2. Instead of 'How was your weekend?' ask 'What was the best part of your weekend?

3. Follow-up with curiosity 'That sounds amazing, how did you get into that?'

QUICK WIN

In your next conversation, ditch a standard question and try a deeper one. Watch how the tone shifts and engagement grows.

Next Steps Make deeper conversations a habit. The more you practice asking and asking deeper questions, the easier it becomes. When you're ready, gradually share more of your thoughts; this models vulnerability and builds mutual trust.

Research Insight Studies show that people who engage in meaningful conversations experience greater happiness, reduced loneliness, and higher social satisfaction[155].

Hack #6:

CREATE A SENSE OF SAFETY – BUILD A SPACE WHERE YOU CAN RECHARGE AND THRIVE

Why it Works: Your living space is more than just a place to sleep. It's an environment where you recharge and feel safe. A secure and comfortable space fosters confidence, creativity and personal growth.

How To Do It

1. Personalise

    - Add decorations like posters, photos, and fairy lights.
    - Use comfortable bedding and cushions.
    - Incorporate plants or greenery.

2. Organise

    - Set up a study area with the necessary supplies.
    - Use storage solutions to minimise clutter.
    - Keep cleaning supplies handy for regular tidying.

3. Establish Routines

    - Set a daily cleaning schedule.
    - Create a study and relaxation timetable.
    - Develop a meal plan and grocery list for efficient shopping.

4. Security

    - Lock your doors and windows when leaving.

- Save emergency contacts.
- Familiarise yourself with campus security protocols.

5. Amenities

- Explore communal spaces like lounges or kitchens.
- Take advantage of any nearby study areas or libraries.
- Utilise maintenance services for repairs or issues.

QUICK WIN

This week, take 10 minutes to declutter your space, to boost focus and reduce stress.

Next Steps Transform your living space into a place where you feel comfortable and in control. Use warm lighting, a comfortable chair or couch, and create distinct zones for work, rest and downtime. A well-organised space can help you think clearly and perform better.

Research Insight People who feel safe and secure in their living environment are more likely to take creative risks, explore new ideas, and experience greater personal growth. A stable environment supports psychological safety - a key factor in self-expression, learning and innovation[156].

Hack #7:
GET OUTSIDE – BOOST YOUR MOOD AND ENERGY IN JUST 10 MINUTES

Why It Works Spending time outdoors does wonders for your mental and physical health. Exposure to natural light and fresh air improves your mood, reduces stress, and boosts creativity.

How To Do It

1. Go for a daily walk: Just 10 minutes increases melatonin and releases endorphins.

2. Bring nature inside: Houseplants remove air pollutants and add moisture to the air.

3. Explore green spaces: Parks, gardens and forests are relaxing.

QUICK WIN

Tomorrow, take a 10-minute walk outside during your lunch break. You'll return refreshed and ready to tackle the rest of the day.

Next Steps Make nature a part of your weekly routine. Schedule a longer walk, hike, or outdoor workout once a week to reconnect with the natural world and clear your mind.

Research Insight In one study, participants who spent just 20 minutes in nature experienced a measurable drop in cortisol levels, even without engaging in exercise or social interaction.[157]

Hack #8:
SHARED SPACES – TURN EVERYDAY MOMENTS INTO NEW CONNECTIONS

Why It Works Proximity fosters connection. Shared spaces – like common rooms, libraries or kitchens – naturally bring people together without pressure or formality.

How to Do It

1. **Be present**: Instead of staying in your room all day, bring your work, meals or downtime into a shared space.

2. **Keep it casual**: You don't have to start a deep conversation. A smile, small talk, or sharing snacks can open the door.

3. **Look for overlap**: Join others who are already there, whether it's for lunch, watching TV or working on assignments.

4. **Respect space**: If someone's studying or relaxing, be mindful; connection grows best with comfort, not pressure.

QUICK WIN

Bring your laptop to a communal area for study time or linger in the kitchen while making a meal. Use these moments to chat with others.

Next Steps Suggest shared activities like a movie night, group cooking, or a game night to create memorable experiences together.

Research Insight Shared spaces in student housing increase opportunities for spontaneous social interaction.[158] All help reduce loneliness and build a sense of belonging.

Hack #9:
VOLUNTEER – FIND PURPOSE AND FRIENDSHIP THROUGH GIVING BACK

Why It Works Helping others gives you a sense of purpose, builds confidence, and creates chances to connect with people who care about the same things you do.

How to Do It

1. **Start small**: You don't need loads of time. Even 1–2 hours a week can make a real difference.

2. **Follow your interests:** Whether it's animals, the environment, education, or mental health, there's something for everyone.

3. **Check your uni's volunteering hub or SU for listings:** Many universities partner with local organisations and charities.

4. **Say yes to one-off events:** It's a great way to try things out and meet new people without a big commitment.

QUICK WIN

Find one volunteering opportunity this week that excites you. Check out university societies or local community boards for ideas.

Next Steps Join regular volunteering groups or societies to build long-term friendships while making a positive difference.

Research Insight Studies show that students who volunteer regularly report significantly improved mental wellbeing, increased life satisfaction and reduced feelings of isolation.[159]

Hack #10:
EAN INTO VULNERABILITY – BUILD DEEPER, STRONGER CONNECTIONS BY BEING REAL

Why It Works Sharing your struggles invites others to do the same. Vulnerability breaks down walls and builds trust, leading to deeper, more meaningful connections.

How to Do It

1. **Start small.** You don't have to overshare. Try opening up about a tough day, a moment of doubt, or something you're finding challenging.

2. **Choose your people.** Begin with someone you trust – someone who listens without judgement.

3. **Use "I feel…" language.** Express what's going on internally instead of just describing external events.

4. **Create space for others, too.** When you're open, it often gives others permission to be real with you.

5. **Be brave.** You'll be surprised how quickly conversations deepen when one person takes the first step.

QUICK WIN

Open up to a trusted friend about something that's been on your mind. It doesn't have to be big, just start small.

Next Steps Make it a habit to check in with friends regularly, creating a mutual space for support, honesty and understanding.

Research Insight Dr Brené Brown's work on vulnerability highlights that authentic sharing fosters deeper connections and reduces feelings of loneliness and shame.[160]

Reflective Questions:

1. Who are the people in your life who make you feel most supported? How can you nurture those relationships?

2. Think about a time you felt truly connected. What made that moment special, and how can you recreate it?

3. Which area of connection do you struggle with most, building friendships, maintaining them or finding a community?

BUILD THE CONNECTIONS THAT MATTER

At the heart of our wellbeing lies the fundamental need for connection – connection with others, with nature and with ourselves. **You need people. And people need you.**

These bonds are not just nice-to-haves; they are essential for thriving. Strong connections buffer stress, boost resilience, and remind us that we are never alone, even when life feels overwhelming. The more you invest in connection, the richer your life becomes, filled with more joy, more purpose and deeper meaning.

This week, take one small step. Send a message, share a moment or simply show up. Because sometimes the smallest gestures create the strongest bonds.

PILLAR 6:

SLEEP

RECLAIM DEEP REST AS

YOUR SUPERPOWER

CHAPTER 16:
SLEEP – THE ULTIMATE ACADEMIC ADVANTAGE

> "Sleep is the Swiss Army knife of health. When sleep is deficient, there is sickness and disease. And when sleep is abundant, there is vitality and health."
>
> Dr. Matthew Walker

Sleep is often the first thing that's sacrificed when university demands pile up. The all-nighter culture, endless binge-watching and caffeine-fuelled cramming sessions make sleep seem like something you can put off, something you'll catch up on later. But what if sleep wasn't just a necessity, but your biggest academic advantage? In this chapter, we'll dig into the biology and purpose of sleep, the science behind sleep cycles, and how reclaiming deep rest can give you an unfair advantage at university and beyond.

THE EVOLUTION OF SLEEP: WHY REST IS WORTH THE RISK

Have you ever wondered why humans, despite being vulnerable to predators, evolved to spend nearly a third of their lives asleep? Lying down, closing your eyes and becoming completely defenceless in the wild seems counterintuitive. So why would evolution prioritise sleep, even when survival was at stake?

The answer lies in the immense benefits sleep provides. The advantages of sleep, physical recovery, mental preparation and energy conservation far outweigh the risks. In fact, sleep became one of the most essential survival tools in our evolutionary arsenal.

Physical Recovery: Deep sleep allowed muscles to repair and injuries to heal. Growth hormones released during this stage of sleep helped early humans stay strong, ready to hunt, escape predators, or endure harsh conditions. Sleep deprivation, on the other hand, left individuals weaker, slower and more prone to illness, a fatal disadvantage in the wild.

Mental Preparedness: REM sleep (Rapid Eye Movement sleep) served as a 'mental training ground.' During this stage, the brain processed memories, simulated scenarios, and rehearsed responses to threats or challenges. Dreaming about evading predators or planning a hunt could improve survival in waking life.

Energy Conservation: Without artificial light, early humans naturally synced with the light-dark cycle (circadian rhythm). Night-time activities were limited and risky, so conserving energy through sleep during these hours made evolutionary sense. It ensured individuals were fully recharged for daytime tasks like foraging, hunting or defending against threats.

Group Safety: Sleeping in groups was another ingenious adaptation. Individuals could take turns keeping watch, allowing others to rest deeply without leaving the group entirely vulnerable. This shared responsibility meant the group as a whole was stronger, sharper and more resilient.

UNDERSTANDING CIRCADIAN RHYTHMS

Every organism has adapted to Earth's 24-hour cycle, and so have you. This natural rhythm, called the circadian rhythm, acts as your internal clock, guiding sleep, energy levels, mood and focus. At the core is your body's 'master clock', the suprachiasmatic nucleus (SCN) in the brain. This tiny cluster of neurons responds directly to light and darkness, synchronising your sleep-wake cycle, hormone release, and body temperature with the time of day. Each organ has its own clock, all working in harmony.

Light = Wakefulness

- When morning light hits your eyes, the SCN signals the release of cortisol, helping you feel alert and ready for the day.

- Natural sunlight also suppresses melatonin, your sleep hormone, reinforcing wakefulness.

Darkness = Sleep Mode

- As daylight fades, your SCN triggers melatonin production, preparing your body for rest.

- Bright screens at night confuse your brain, delaying melatonin release and disrupting deep sleep.

In Spain, siestas, short afternoon naps, are a cherished tradition, often linked to recharging after a midday meal. But did you know that in Japan, inemuri, or 'sleeping on the job', is not just accepted but sometimes encouraged? Inemuri translates to 'being present while asleep' and is often seen as a sign of hard work and dedication.[161]

HIGH ACHIEVER SLEEP SECRETS: WHAT TOP PERFORMERS KNOW ABOUT REST

What do LeBron James, Emma Watson and Jeff Bezos have in common? They prioritise sleep, not just as rest, but as their secret weapon for success.

- LeBron James averages 12 hours of sleep a day, combining full nights with long naps to support performance, recovery, and mental sharpness.[162]

- Jeff Bezos guards his 8 hours of sleep religiously, crediting it with improved decision-making and clearer thinking.[163]

- Emma Watson and Taylor Swift have both spoken about how sleep fuels their creativity, resilience and mental wellbeing.

If the world's most successful people rely on sleep to stay at the top of their game, imagine what it could do for your focus, energy and academic performance.

Why Sleep is Your Ultimate Academic Superpower

Sleep isn't a luxury; it's the key to unlocking academic excellence. Your ability to learn, focus and retain information depends on sleep.

Sleep Enhances Mental Performance

- **Better grades:** Research consistently shows that students who sleep 7–9 hours per night outperform those who don't.[164] Sleep strengthens memory, consolidates knowledge, and enhances problem-solving skills – all crucial for academic success.

- **Faster learning:** Pulling an all-nighter to cram for an exam might seem productive, but it backfires. Sleep is when your brain processes and stores the information you've studied. Without it, your retention and recall suffer.

- **Sharper focus:** Struggling to concentrate in lectures? Sleep clears brain fog and boosts attention span, so you're ready to tackle your to-do list with laser focus.

Sleep Fuels Your Physical and Emotional Health

- **Boosted mental health:** Lack of sleep makes you more vulnerable to stress, anxiety, and depression. Consistent high-quality sleep builds emotional resilience and helps you manage daily pressures more effectively.

- **Stronger immune system:** Skipping sleep makes you more likely to catch the cold that's going around campus. Your immune system relies on deep sleep to fight off infections and recover from illness.

- **More energy for social life and hobbies:** Sleep gives you the stamina to balance coursework, social events, and extracurriculars. A well-rested you means more time for fun.

THE 4 STAGES OF SLEEP (AND WHY THEY MATTER FOR YOU)

Each night, your body moves through several stages of sleep, each with a specific purpose. A full sleep cycle lasts about 90 minutes, and most people complete 4–6 cycles per night. Here's what happens:

Stage 1: Light Sleep (NREM 1) – The Transition Phase

- **What happens:** This brief stage (5–10 minutes) is when your body shifts from wakefulness to sleep. Breathing slows, and brain waves transition to alpha and theta patterns.

- **Why it matters:** It acts as a gateway to deeper sleep, helping you transition into the restorative stages that follow.

- **Fun fact:** Ever felt like you were falling as you doze off? That 'hypnic jerk' happens here!

Stage 2: Stabilising Sleep (NREM 2) – Memory Consolidation Mode

- **What happens:** Your body temperature drops, heart rate slows, and brain activity features 'sleep spindles', brief bursts that help consolidate memories.

- **Why it matters:** This stage makes up 50% of total sleep and is essential for learning, problem-solving and nervous system balance.

- **Fun fact:** Sleep spindles help your brain 'lock in' information, perfect for remembering lecture notes!

Stage 3: Deep Sleep (NREM 3) – The Physical Recharge

- **What happens:** Your brain waves slow to delta waves, the deepest and slowest state. Growth hormones are released, and the immune system kicks into high gear to repair and regenerate the body.

- **Why it matters:** This is prime recovery time for your body and brain. It's when toxins are flushed out and muscles recover, which is crucial after all-nighters or gym sessions.

- **Fun fact:** Ever woken up feeling groggy and disoriented? That's called sleep inertia, and it happens when you're forced out of deep sleep too early.

Stage 4: REM Sleep – The Brainpower Booster

- **What happens:** Brain activity spikes, vivid dreams occur, and your body enters temporary paralysis to prevent you from acting out those dreams.

- **Why it matters:** REM sleep is essential for creativity, emotional regulation and complex problem-solving, all key skills for students juggling deadlines and exams.

- **Fun fact:** Scientist Otto Loewi dreamed of an experiment, woke up to jot it down and later won the Nobel Prize in Medicine because of it.

If you're short on time, aim to wake up at the end of one of the 90-minute sleep cycles (rather than waking mid-cycle). You'll feel refreshed, avoid grogginess and have maximised the benefits of whatever sleep you manage to get.

TAILORED SLEEP ADVICE FOR STUDENTS

Aligning your sleep habits with your academic needs gives you a significant advantage, not just in academics but in every aspect of university life. Different fields of study demand unique skills, and sleep can be the secret ingredient to unlocking your potential.

STEM Students: The Logic Masters

If you're in a technical field like mathematics, physics, engineering or computer science, your work revolves around logical reasoning and problem-solving. Sleep is the hidden force behind your brain's ability to crack complex equations, spot patterns, and approach challenges with innovative solutions. **Deep sleep for logical thinking:** This stage of sleep consolidates factual knowledge, strengthening your ability to solve equations, debug code or analyse data with precision. **REM sleep for innovative problem-solving:** During REM sleep, your brain combines creativity with logic, often connecting seemingly unrelated ideas to spark novel solutions. Recharge your brain with a 20-minute power nap during the day. Short naps improve cognitive function and give you the boost needed to tackle logical tasks.

Creative Fields: The Innovators and Dreamers

If you're studying design, writing, music or the arts, sleep is your secret weapon for creativity. REM sleep helps your brain process and synthesise ideas in unexpected ways. **REM sleep and creativity:** This stage enables your brain to form connections and process information in ways that aren't possible while awake. It's why dream-inspired ideas often lead to groundbreaking work. **Dream inspiration:** Many artists and creators credit their dreams with their greatest works. Paul McCartney dreamed the melody for 'Yesterday', and Salvador Dalí famously used his dreams to inspire his surrealist masterpieces. **Feeling stuck on a project?** Instead of pulling an all-nighter, prioritise sleep. You'll wake up with a fresh perspective and the clarity to move forward.

Keep a notebook or journal by your bed. Write down any dreams, sketches or ideas as soon as you wake up, dreams fade quickly, but even a small note can spark a creative breakthrough later.

Healthcare, Education and Social Science Students: The Empaths

If you're studying nursing, psychology, education or sociology, your work often requires a balance of empathy, critical thinking and effective communication. Sleep enhances these vital skills, making you better equipped to navigate emotionally demanding tasks. **Emotional regulation:** REM sleep helps process emotions, improving empathy and interpersonal skills. **Critical thinking:** Deep sleep strengthens neural connections that support reasoning and decision-making. Practise mindfulness before bed to relax your mind and enhance emotional regulation. If you're juggling night shifts, use blackout curtains or an eye mask to simulate darkness during the day and limit blue light exposure to protect your sleep cycle.

Business and Law Students: The Strategists

If you're studying business or law, your success depends on sharp decision-making, analytical thinking and persuasive communication. Sleep plays a critical role in sharpening these abilities. **Sharper decision-making:** REM sleep enhances strategic thinking by allowing your brain to weigh options and make sound decisions. **Improved persuasion:** A well-rested brain boosts your ability to construct compelling arguments and negotiate effectively. Build a regular sleep routine to support your brain's ability to think critically and strategically, even during very stressful times.

Essay Deadlines and Exam Prep: Sleep Your Way to Success

Every student knows the pain of pulling an all-nighter before an essay deadline or exam. But the truth is, sleep trumps last-minute cramming. **Memory recall:** Sleep strengthens the hippocampus, converting short-term memories into long-term knowledge. If you study today and sleep well tonight, you'll remember far more tomorrow. **Sharper focus and reduced stress:** A well-rested brain is better equipped to focus, think clearly and manage exam anxiety. End your study sessions at least an hour before bed. Let your brain unwind to consolidate information while you sleep.

By tailoring your sleep habits to the demands of your field, you're not just prioritising rest – you're giving yourself a strategic edge in your academic and personal life. Sleep smarter, not harder, and watch how it transforms your ability to thrive.

The 'Sleep Bank' Myth: Many students believe they can 'catch up' on sleep over the weekend, but sleep doesn't work like a bank. Consistent sleep deprivation disrupts physiological functions over time, leading to cumulative deficits that can't be fully 'repaid'. Regular high-quality sleep allows each stage to conduct its essential work.

SLEEP'S ROLE IN HORMONE REGULATION AND HOMEOSTASIS

Sleep is essential for maintaining hormonal balance, which affects mood, metabolism, immune function and overall physical health. During sleep, the body regulates several hormones critical to wellbeing.

Growth hormone: Released predominantly during deep sleep, this is essential for tissue growth, muscle repair, and cell regeneration. For those who engage in physical activities, this helps them recover from exercise while maintaining overall physical health.

Cortisol: The body's primary stress hormone is regulated during sleep. As morning approaches, cortisol levels rise, helping us wake. Chronic sleep deprivation disrupts this.

Leptin and ghrelin: These hormones regulate hunger and satiety, influenced by sleep. Leptin signals fullness, while ghrelin triggers hunger. When sleep-deprived, the body produces less leptin and more ghrelin, leading to increased appetite and cravings, particularly for high-calorie foods. This imbalance contributes to weight gain, fatigue, and metabolic issues.

SLEEP IS YOUR COMPETITIVE EDGE

You wouldn't expect your phone to function at 5% battery, so why would you expect your brain to perform on limited sleep?

The best students, top athletes, and most successful professionals all prioritise sleep because they know it's their secret weapon. Prioritise rest, not just as recovery, but as a tool for academic and personal success. Because sleep isn't wasted time, it's the key to unlocking your full potential.

CHAPTER 17:

SLEEP CHALLENGES AT UNI

"The way to a more productive, inspired, and joyful life is getting enough sleep."

Arianna Huffington

It's 11pm. You tell yourself, just one more episode, just five more minutes on TikTok, and suddenly, it's nearly morning. Your alarm blares, and you're dragging yourself out of bed, promising you'll sleep early tonight. But then... the cycle repeats.

University life is a whirlwind of independence, academic pressure and social opportunities. The freedom to set your own schedule can be exciting, but it often comes at the cost of sleep. With constant deadlines, late-night study sessions, and the ever-present lure of technology, getting enough rest can feel impossible. However, understanding how stress and technology affect sleep is the first step towards taking control and improving both academic performance and overall wellbeing.

TECHNOLOGY: THE SLEEP THIEF

In a world designed to keep people constantly engaged, sleep often becomes a casualty. Streaming services, social media platforms, and endless notifications compete for attention well into the night. Even Netflix's CEO has openly admitted that their biggest competitor is sleep, proving that these platforms are engineered to keep users watching, scrolling and engaging far longer than they originally intended.[165]

One of the primary reasons technology disrupts sleep is the exposure to blue light. Phones, laptops and tablets emit blue light, which interferes with melatonin production, the hormone responsible for making you feel sleepy. Under normal circumstances, melatonin levels rise in the evening, helping the body wind down and prepare for rest. However, when blue light is absorbed through the eyes, the brain is tricked into believing it is still daytime. This delays melatonin release and pushes back the body's natural sleep cycle, later and later. This effect goes beyond simply delaying sleep. Prolonged exposure reduces the amount of REM sleep, the stage of sleep crucial for memory retention, problem-solving and emotional regulation.[166] Many assume that switching from a phone to an e-reader before bed is harmless, but unfortunately, e-readers are not innocent either. Like phones, they also emit blue light.

The problem isn't just how technology affects sleep, but also how poor sleep increases dependence on technology. When you're sleep-deprived, daytime fatigue and lack of focus push you to seek stimulation, often through caffeine, energy drinks and more screen time. This reinforces the cycle of exhaustion and overstimulation, making it even harder to break free. **Students who sleep fewer than six hours a night often perform as poorly on cognitive tasks as someone who is drunk.**[167]

HOW ARTIFICIAL LIGHT DISRUPTS SLEEP

Since the 1950s, the widespread availability of affordable artificial lighting has fundamentally changed human sleep patterns. Unlike our ancestors, who followed the natural rise and fall of the sun, modern life extends wakefulness long past nightfall with bright indoor lighting and screen exposure. Research has shown that when people are in environments free from artificial light, they tend to fall asleep and wake up in sync with the sun.

A study by the University of Colorado Boulder found that participants who spent a week camping without artificial light experienced a significant shift in their sleep patterns. By the end of the week, their melatonin levels began rising nearly two hours earlier in the evening than before, allowing them to fall asleep sooner and wake up feeling more refreshed. But what would happen if all light, natural and artificial, was removed? Experiments led by chronobiologist Michel Siffre in the 1960s explored this question by placing people in caves with no exposure to light. Surprisingly, their sleep-wake cycles began to lengthen, sometimes to 25 or even 48 hours. This demonstrated that while light is a primary regulator of sleep, the body also has an internal clock, one that can function independently, but not as efficiently.

These studies highlight the powerful role of light in sleep regulation, demonstrating that too much artificial light delays sleep, while too little external light can disrupt our natural rhythm altogether. Limiting artificial light exposure in the evening, dimming indoor lighting, and reducing screen time before bed helps restore a healthier sleep cycle, without needing to camp in the wilderness or isolate in a cave.

THE PHONE PROBLEM: MORE THAN JUST BLUE LIGHT

It's not just the blue light disrupting your sleep; it's the constant connectivity keeping your mind on high alert. Even if you're not actively using it, just having your phone in the bedroom can impact your sleep. The mere presence of your phone nearby can increase feelings of alertness, making it harder to fully relax and drift off.

Why? Because your brain knows the phone is there, packed with messages, notifications, and endless entertainment, waiting to pull you back in. This is the attention economy at work, tech companies design apps to hijack your focus, keeping you engaged for as long as possible. The result? A restless mind, shorter sleep cycles, and chronic fatigue

THE CULTURE OF SLEEP DEPRIVATION AT UNI

Over 70% of students don't get the recommended 7-9 hours of sleep each night.[168] Sleep deprivation is often seen as a badge of honour. There's an unspoken competition over who can pull the most all-nighters or get by on the fewest hours of sleep. Productivity is glorified, while sleep is dismissed as a luxury rather than a necessity. Yet, research shows that students who consistently sleep fewer than six hours struggle with memory, focus and decision-making. Pulling all-nighters may feel productive in the moment, but it harms long-term academic performance.

THE CONSEQUENCE OF SLEEP DEPRIVATION ON ACADEMIC PERFORMANCE

Sleep is essential for memory consolidation. Without enough sleep, what you study during late-night sessions may not be retained effectively. The prefrontal cortex, which controls executive functions like planning and problem-solving, becomes less effective when you're tired, too. This makes it harder to stay focused, solve complex problems, and retain information, leading to more mistakes and difficulty with even simple tasks. Sleep-deprived students have a 40% reduction in their ability to retain new information compared to well-rested students. This means that even if you're studying longer, you're not retaining as much knowledge. This creates a cycle: poor sleep leads to lower academic performance, which causes more stress and worsens sleep.

BUSTING SLEEP MYTHS

Myth: 'I can train my body to function on less sleep.'

Reality: While you might think you're adapting to getting 5 or fewer hours of sleep a night, your cognitive and physical performance is still declining, even if you no longer feel as tired. Research shows that chronic sleep deprivation leads to long-term deficits in memory, attention and decision-making.[169]

Why it matters: Students who sacrifice sleep for late-night studying may find their efforts counterproductive as their ability to retain information and think critically declines.

Think an hour of lost sleep doesn't matter? When we lose just one hour of sleep during daylight saving in March, heart attack rates spike the next day.[170] This highlights how even minor disruptions to your sleep can have serious effects on your body and brain. Pulling an all-nighter might feel harmless, but it's a reminder that sleep deprivation affects far more than your energy levels; it impacts your focus, memory and long-term health.

Myth: 'Napping Can Replace Nighttime Sleep.'

Reality: While power naps of 15–20 minutes can provide a temporary energy boost, they cannot compensate for the loss of deep or REM sleep that happens at night. Deep sleep and REM sleep require extended, uninterrupted periods of rest to occur, and these stages are essential for physical recovery and memory consolidation.

Why it matters: Over-reliance on naps can disrupt your natural sleep cycle, making it harder to fall asleep at night and worsening sleep deprivation.

Use naps strategically. A short nap early in the afternoon can recharge your brain, but avoid napping too close to bedtime to ensure it doesn't interfere with your nightly rest.

Did you know? Studies show that students who sleep fewer than 6 hours a night are 40% more likely to experience academic burnout.[171]

MODERN DISRUPTION: WHY WE'RE MORE SLEEP DEPRIVED THAN EVER

Today, our bodies still rely on these ancient rhythms, but modern life has thrown them out of sync. Instead of respecting natural light cycles, we flood our evenings with artificial light from screens. Blue light, in particular, disrupts melatonin production, the very hormone our ancestors relied on to signal bedtime.

And while our ancestors rested in complete darkness and silence, many of us sleep with interruptions from phones, notifications, and noisy environments. These modern 'predators' attack our sleep, leaving us stressed, tired, and less resilient. Routinely sleeping less than six or seven hours doubles your risk of cancer and wrecks your immune system.[172]

Did you know? **Research suggests that over 50% of people diagnosed with ADHD may have an underlying sleep disorder that goes unnoticed.**[173] This could mean that your inability to focus in lectures, restlessness during study sessions, or constant mental fog, symptoms often blamed on ADHD or stress, might stem from poor sleep.

BREAKING THE CYCLE: SMALL CHANGES = BIG IMPACT

It's time to reframe Sleep. Sleep is not wasted time; it's an evolutionary superpower that enhances your ability to thrive. The good news is you can take steps to improve your sleep and break the cycle of deprivation. Prioritising sleep might require some adjustments, but the benefits are worth it. By making small changes to your sleep habits, you're not only boosting your academic performance but also supporting your mental and physical health, helping you thrive at university and beyond.

CHAPTER 18:

DEVELOPING HEALTHY SLEEP HABITS FOR ACADEMIC ACHIEVEMENT

> "You will perform better, make better decisions, and have a better body when you get the sleep you require."
>
> *Shawn Stevenson*

Uni is busy. Between late-night study sessions, meeting deadlines, and trying to squeeze in a social life, sleep often falls down the priority list. As we have explored in the past few chapters, prioritising quality sleep could be your secret weapon for academic success. Sleep isn't just about feeling rested; it's the foundation for everything, from your ability to concentrate in lectures, to managing stress, to staying physically and mentally healthy.

Imagine waking up fully energised and mentally sharp, ready to crush the day ahead. The good news? You don't need to overhaul your entire life to do so. In this chapter, I'll share practical sleep hacks that are easy to fit into your busy schedule. For this, keep your eyes open!

Hack #1:
GET MORNING SUNLIGHT – RESET YOUR ENERGY AND SLEEP NATURALLY

Why It Works: Morning sunlight helps reset your circadian rhythm, your internal clock, boosting energy and preparing your body for better sleep.

When your eyes absorb natural light in the morning, it triggers the release of cortisol, the hormone that boosts alertness, focus and motivation. Unlike the stress-induced spikes of cortisol that can cause anxiety, this morning cortisol boost is beneficial; it helps wake you up naturally, improves mood and enhances cognitive function. At the same time, morning light suppresses melatonin, the sleep hormone, ensuring its proper release later in the evening. This natural cycle promotes better sleep quality, sharper thinking and higher productivity.

How to Do It

1. Spend 10–15 minutes outside or near a sunny window within an hour of waking.

2. Pair your morning coffee, tea or breakfast with outdoor time, even if it's just sitting near an open window.

3. No sunlight? Use an LED light ring or a bright light to mimic natural sunlight and signal wakefulness to your brain.

QUICK WIN

Tomorrow morning, sit by a window while drinking your first coffee or tea.

Research Insight: Studies show that morning light exposure improves sleep quality, regulates circadian rhythms, reduces symptoms of depression, and enhances cognitive function.[174]

Hack #2:
CREATE A SLEEP SANCTUARY – TRANSFORM YOUR SPACE INTO A REST HAVEN

Why It Works: A cool, dark and quiet room signals to your body it's time to rest. These conditions mirror the environment our ancestors relied on for safety and recovery.

When your sleeping environment mimics these natural conditions, your body responds by entering sleep more easily and staying asleep longer. Darkness triggers the production of melatonin, the sleep hormone, while a cooler temperature promotes physical recovery and prevents overheating during the night. Silence (or soothing sounds) allows your brain to relax without constant alerts of potential threats, a key survival mechanism from our evolutionary past.

How to do it:

1. Keep your room between 16–19°C.

2. Block out light with blackout curtains or a sleep mask.

3. Mask disruptive sounds with earplugs or experiment with white, pink, green, or brown noise to find what relaxes you most.

4. Remove electronics and unnecessary clutter from your sleep space.

The Power of Sound

Not all noise is disruptive; some sounds can enhance sleep quality by masking sudden disturbances and helping your brain settle into a relaxed state.

- **White noise**: A steady sound containing all frequencies at equal intensity, like a fan, air conditioner or static. It's great for blocking background noise.

- **Pink noise**: A deeper, more natural-sounding variation of white noise, similar to rainfall or ocean waves. Research suggests it can improve deep sleep and memory.

- **Green noise**: A softer, mid-frequency noise that mimics nature, like a distant river or rustling leaves. It's ideal for relaxation and stress relief.

- **Brown noise**: Deeper than pink noise, resembling thunder or a low waterfall. Many people find it the most calming, especially for focus or anxiety.

With the right type of background sound, you can create a soothing sleep environment that drowns out distractions and helps you drift off faster and stay asleep longer.

QUICK WIN

Tonight, choose one simple upgrade: close your curtains tighter, grab earplugs, or set up a fan for gentle background noise.

Next Steps: Experiment with different natural sound options:

1. A fan or an air purifier creates a steady background hum
2. A humidifier or a white noise machine, if you already have one, can double as a noise blocker
3. A radio or a speaker with a sleep timer, tune into static or a quiet nature station
4. A DIY noise machine, a small tabletop fountain, or a ticking clock can create soothing ambient sounds

Research Insight: Students living in darker, noise-reduced rooms reported better sleep quality, deeper rest, and sharper mental clarity during the day[175].

Hack #3:
CREATE A CONSISTENT SLEEP SCHEDULE – SET YOUR BODY'S NATURAL ALARM CLOCK

Why It Works Going to bed and waking up at the same time every day is like setting your body's alarm clock. It helps you fall asleep faster, stay asleep longer, and wake up feeling refreshed, even if you've had a late night. Consistency strengthens your circadian rhythm, making it easier to get quality sleep without tossing and turning.

How to Do It

1. Aim for 7–9 hours of sleep each night.

2. Adjust your bedtime by 15-minute increments until it fits with your ideal schedule.

3. Stick to your chosen wake-up time even on weekends to maintain your circadian rhythm.

QUICK WIN

Pick just one consistent wake-up time to start. Once that's a habit, adjust your bedtime gradually.

Research Insight Students with consistent sleep and wake times perform better academically and report higher levels of energy and focus compared to those with irregular sleep schedules.

'We're competing with sleep, and we're winning.'[176] **Netflix CEO**

Hack #4:
BINGE, SNOOZE, REPEAT – BREAK THE CYCLE FOR BETTER SLEEP

Why it Works We've all faced the epic battle of 'just one more episode' versus bedtime. Your favourite show ends on a cliffhanger, and Netflix tempts you with that five-second countdown to the next episode. Before you know it, it's 3 a.m. and your 8 a.m. lecture feels like a distant dream. And then there's the snooze button struggle. You set your alarm optimistically, promising yourself you'll wake up on time, only to hit snooze three (or five) times, convincing yourself that seven more minutes will somehow make a difference. Sound familiar?

How To Do It

1. Set a firm "screen cut-off time" at least 30–60 minutes before bed.

2. Place your phone or alarm across the room to force yourself to physically get up in the morning.

3. If you must use screens at night, wear blue light-blocking glasses to reduce melatonin disruption.

QUICK WIN

Tonight, set your alarm across the room and commit to getting up as soon as it goes off.

Research Insight Evening exposure to blue light, especially from phones, tablets, and laptops, delays melatonin production, shortens sleep duration, and increases daytime fatigue, especially in young adults[177].

Hack #5:
PREPARE FOR TOMORROW TONIGHT – CALM YOUR MIND BEFORE BED

Why It Works: Planning for the next day reduces anxiety and helps your brain shift into relaxation mode. By addressing tomorrow's tasks in advance, you minimise late-night overthinking and create a sense of control, allowing you to sleep more peacefully.

How to Do It

1. Spend 10–15 minutes before bed writing down your to-do list for tomorrow.

2. Lay out your clothes, pack your bag, or prepare meals for the next day.

3. Use a journal to reflect on one positive thing from the day to shift your mindset towards gratitude and calm.

QUICK WIN

Tonight, before climbing into bed, write down three things you want to accomplish tomorrow. Pair it with light stretches or a few slow deep breaths to help your body and mind relax even further.

Research Insight Students who write detailed to-do lists before bed fall asleep faster and experience significantly fewer sleep disruptions during the night. Offloading tomorrow's tasks onto paper helps calm a racing mind and promotes deeper, more restful sleep[178].

Hack #6:
AVOID CAFFEINE IN THE AFTERNOON – PROTECT YOUR SLEEP HIDDEN STIMULI

Why It Works Caffeine stays in your system for hours, potentially disrupting your ability to fall asleep later. It has a half-life of about 5–6 hours, meaning that if you drink a coffee with 100mg of caffeine at 4 p.m., around 50mg will still be in your system by 10 p.m., and 25mg by 4 a.m.. Since complete metabolism can take 8–12 hours, even an afternoon cup can interfere with your ability to get into deep, restorative sleep.

How to Do It

1. Avoid coffee, energy drinks, or caffeinated tea after midday.

2. Swap them for herbal teas like chamomile, peppermint, or rooibos, or choose decaf options.

3. If you need a pick-me-up, try a quick walk outside for a natural energy boost instead of reaching for caffeine.

QUICK WIN

Tomorrow, replace your usual afternoon coffee with a caffeine-free herbal tea, or get outside for a short walk instead.

Next Steps Try it every other day until your body adjusts, you'll likely notice better sleep (and fewer afternoon energy crashes) sooner than you expect.

Research Insight Consuming caffeine even six hours before bedtime can reduce total sleep time by more than an hour, often without the person even realising their sleep was disrupted. Caffeine delays melatonin production, making it harder to fall asleep, even if you feel tired[179].

Hack #7:
TIME YOUR MEALS FOR BETTER SLEEP – LET YOUR BODY WIND DOWN NATURALLY

Why It Works The timing of your last meal directly affects your blood sugar levels and energy balance as you wind down for the night. Eating too close to bedtime keeps your digestive system active when your body should be preparing for deep rest, making it harder to fall asleep and reducing overall sleep quality.

How to Do It

1. Finish eating at least 2–3 hours before bed to allow full digestion.

2. Choose a balanced dinner with protein, healthy fats, and fibre to prevent blood sugar spikes or crashes that may wake you up at night.

3. Avoid heavy, spicy, or sugary foods in the evening, which can interfere with digestion and sleep quality.

QUICK WIN

Tomorrow, aim to eat dinner earlier and swap sugary desserts for something lighter, like a piece of fruit or a calming herbal tea.

Next Steps Gradually shift your dinner time earlier by 15 minutes each evening until you find the sweet spot that fits your schedule and supports better sleep.

Research Insight Just one week of moderate sleep deprivation can disrupt insulin sensitivity so significantly that your body may temporarily function in a pre-diabetic state.[180]

Hack #8:
KEEP YOUR BED FOR SLEEP ONLY

Why It Works Your brain forms strong associations between environments and behaviours.

When you reserve your bed exclusively for sleep and relaxation and not for studying, scrolling, or eating, your brain automatically recognises it as a cue to wind down and prepare for rest.

How to Do It?

1. Avoid studying, watching TV, eating or working in bed.

2. Reserve your bed for sleep and genuine relaxation only (like quiet reading or mindfulness).

3. Set up a separate study zone, even if it's just a small desk or a different corner of your room.

QUICK WIN

Tonight, try removing one non-sleep-related item, like your laptop, textbooks, or snacks, from your bed to start reinforcing the "sleep-only" association.

Next Steps Over time, your brain will begin to associate your bed with restfulness, making it easier to switch off at night, without needing melatonin or endless scrolling to wind down.

Research Insight Students who create a clear mental association between bed and sleep show significantly faster sleep onset and better sleep quality. This principle is a core strategy in cognitive behavioural therapy for insomnia[181].

Hack #9:
EXERCISE DURING THE DAY – MOVE YOUR BODY, IMPROVE YOUR SLEEP

Why It Works Daytime physical activity reduces stress hormones, boosts endorphins and helps your body transition into deep, restorative sleep at night.

However, timing matters: exercise too late in the evening, and the post-workout adrenaline spike can make it harder to fall asleep.

How to Do It

1. Aim for 20–30 minutes of moderate exercise earlier in the day, like brisk walking, jogging, cycling, or a fitness class.

2. Avoid intense workouts within 2 hours of bedtime.

QUICK WIN

Tomorrow, you could try scheduling a short workout before lunch, even a brisk 15-minute walk between lectures, can significantly improve sleep quality.

Research Insight Regular daytime exercise is linked to faster sleep onset, better sleep quality, and longer total sleep duration, especially when performed in the morning or early afternoon[182].

Hack #10:
CREATE A SENSORY WIND-DOWN RITUAL – SIGNAL TO YOUR BODY IT'S TIME TO SLEEP

Why It Works: Engaging your senses with calming cues signals to your brain that it's time to shift from high alert to relaxation mode.

Soothing lighting, sounds, and scents help transition you into the parasympathetic "rest and digest" state that is essential for sleep.

How to Do It

1. Use dim lighting or warm-toned bulbs an hour before bed to signal to your body that it's time to wind down.

2. Introduce calming scents like lavender or chamomile with essential oils, pillow sprays to create a relaxing atmosphere.

3. Play natural sounds like rainfall, ocean waves or a crackling fire to help your mind switch off.

QUICK WIN

Tonight, dim your lights and try a light mist of lavender on your pillow 30 minutes before bed.

Research Insight: Scent-based rituals like aromatherapy have been shown to significantly reduce heart rate and cortisol levels, promoting deeper, faster sleep[183].

Recovery After Poor Sleep

If you've had a bad night's sleep, don't panic — small steps can help reset your body quickly:

- **Hydrate:** Start your day with water to help your body recover.
- **Get morning sunlight:** Reset your circadian rhythm by stepping outside early.
- Limit caffeine the following day.
- **Take a power nap:** A 15–20-minute nap can recharge you without making you groggy.
- **Eat wisely:** Focus on nutrient-rich foods to stabilise your energy.
- Stick to your usual bedtime to avoid disrupting your sleep cycle further.

What to Do When You Can't Sleep

Lying awake in bed, staring at the ceiling, and willing yourself to sleep only makes things worse. Instead of fighting insomnia, try these science-backed strategies to reset your mind and body for sleep.

Step 1: Get Out of Bed

If you can't fall asleep within 20 minutes, don't just lie there. Get up and do a calming activity like reading, journaling, or light stretching in dim lighting. This prevents your brain from associating your bed with frustration and wakefulness.

Step 2: Try the 4-7-8 Breathing Method

This breathing technique activates the parasympathetic nervous system, calming your heart rate and signalling to your brain that it's safe to sleep.

1. Inhale through your nose for **4 seconds.**
2. Hold your breath for **7 seconds.**
3. Exhale slowly through your mouth for **8 seconds.**
4. Repeat **4–5 times.**

Step 3: Listen to Binaural Beats or Nature Sounds

Low-frequency sounds like ocean waves, rain, or binaural beats can sync brainwave activity with sleep states, helping you drift off naturally.

Step 4: Cool Down Your Body

Your core temperature needs to drop for optimal sleep. Try:

- Keeping your bedroom between 15–19°C.
- Sticking one foot outside the blanket (this helps regulate body temperature).
- Splashing cold water on your face or wrists.

Step 5: Use the 'Cognitive Shuffle'

Racing thoughts keep many people awake. Instead of stressing over tomorrow, distract your brain by imagining random, unrelated words (e.g. apple, mountain, paperclip). This prevents overthinking and mimics the mental drift that naturally happens before sleep.

QUICK WIN

If you're still awake after trying these, repeat Step 1. Avoid looking at the clock, it only adds stress! Trust that sleep will come when your body is ready.

Make Sleep Your Superpower

Sleep isn't just a nice-to-have; it's your secret weapon for success at university. From sharper focus and better grades to improved mental and physical health, the benefits of quality sleep are undeniable. By implementing these practical hacks and rethinking your sleep priorities, you're investing in your future.

Start small, choose one or two hacks to try tonight. Whether it's setting a consistent bedtime, reducing screen time, or simply making your room a bit darker, these tiny changes will ripple into powerful results.

Because sleep isn't wasted time, it's the foundation of everything you're here to achieve.

YOUR 14 DAY THRIVE MODE PLAN

This book may be closing, but your story is just beginning. Every small choice you make, every habit you build, every moment you show up for yourself, it all adds up. This is the heart of Thrive Mode.

BUILD YOUR PERSONAL THRIVE TOOLKIT, ONE DAY AT A TIME

This 14-day plan is designed to help you integrate the six pillars of THRIVE MODE - Mind, Breathe, Move, Fuel, Connect, and Sleep - into your daily life in a simple, manageable way.

This isn't about rigid rules or perfection. It's about small, intentional steps that make a real difference. Each day, you'll try one practical action that strengthens your body, calms your mind, or supports your wellbeing, often in a few minutes.

By the end of two weeks, you'll have built a personalised **Thrive Toolkit** you can carry forward into university life and beyond.

CONCLUSION: THRIVING BEYOND UNIVERSITY

Congratulations, you haven't just finished a book; you've unlocked your THRIVE MODE journey. This isn't just about surviving university, it's about taking control of your wellbeing and designing a life where you don't just survive but truly thrive.

Think back to when you first picked up this book. Perhaps you felt stuck, overwhelmed by academic expectations, or unsure about how to manage being a university student. Now, look at where you are. You're armed with tools empowering you to breathe deeply, move with purpose, sleep well, fuel your body and mind, and connect with yourself and others. These aren't just habits, they're your lifelines. They're the consistent choices carrying you through the highs and lows of life long after you've graduated.

THRIVING IS THE JOURNEY, NOT THE DESTINATION

Thriving isn't about perfection. It's about persistence. It's not about nailing every habit, never feeling stressed, or having all the answers. It's about showing up for yourself, day after day, even when it's hard. It's about knowing how to recalibrate when life feels off-balance.

University is a training ground; it challenges you to grow, adapt and discover who you are. But this is just the beginning. The pillars of THRIVE MODE will continue to guide you, whether you're preparing for your first job interview, building new relationships, or navigating unexpected challenges.

IMAGINE THE POSIBILITIES

Picture your future self. You're not just getting by, you're thriving. When challenges arise (and they will), you have a toolkit to rely on. A deep breath before a big presentation. A restorative walk when stress feels overwhelming. A conversation with a friend reminds you of your connection. These aren't just hypothetical moments. They're

CONCLUSION

your future reality built on habits you've planted here. The choices you make today take root, shaping the person you are blossoming into.

THE RIPPLE EFFECT OF THRIVING

When you thrive, you inspire others. Your energy, resilience, and optimism become contagious. By prioritising your wellbeing and showing up authentically, you create a ripple effect, empowering those around you to do the same.

Whether it's sharing a tip from this book with a friend, encouraging someone to join you on a walk, or embodying the calm and clarity you've cultivated, your actions have the power to create change beyond yourself.

THRIVING TOGETHER

You're not alone in this journey. As you embrace THRIVE MODE, you become part of a larger movement, a community of individuals choosing to prioritise their wellbeing in a world often demanding otherwise. Together, we redefine what it means to succeed. We create a culture where health, connection, and happiness are the foundations, not the afterthought.

ONE STEP AT A TIME

Remember, it's the small, consistent steps which lead to lasting change. Start where you are, with what you have. Take one deep breath. Go for a walk. Make one meaningful connection. Build on these moments and watch how they transform your life.

When life gets busy or overwhelming, return to the **Six Pillars**. Use them as your compass, your guide back to balance. Thriving isn't about doing everything perfectly; it's about making choices that support your growth.

TIPS FOR SUCCESS

1. **Be flexible:** Life happens. If you miss a day or activity, don't stress, just pick up where you left off.

2. **Track your progress:** Keep a journal to note how different practices affect your mood, energy, and focus.

3. **Adjust as needed:** If something doesn't resonate, tweak it or swap it for a practice that aligns better with your goals.

4. **Involve others:** Share your plan with friends or family for extra accountability and encouragement.

5. **Celebrate wins:** Every step forward, big or small, matters. Recognise and celebrate your progress daily.

Congratulations on everything you've accomplished so far. This is just the beginning. Now, go out there and live boldly, live fully and thrive.

Ready for your next step? Keep thriving with us...

ABOUT THE AUTHOR

Philippa Charrier is redefining how we think about student wellbeing by focusing on the spaces where we live, learn, and grow. In a sector where wellbeing is often treated as a tick-box exercise, she shows how design, science, and lived experience can transform everyday environments into places that actively support mental health, connection, and performance.

A wellbeing advocate, property developer, and co-founder of the award-winning student housing company **FAT Properties**, Philippa designs accommodation with mental health and human potential at the forefront. After witnessing the rising tide of burnout, anxiety, and loneliness among students, both as a housing provider and as a mum, she made it her mission to change the student experience from the inside out.

She co-authored the bestselling book *Designed for Wellbeing* and has worked with universities, developers, and wellbeing experts to pioneer science-backed spaces that support success from the ground up.

Her latest book, *Student Thrive Mode: How to Hack Your Mind & Body for University Success*, is her personal manifesto, an empowering call to action for students to take charge of their wellbeing, unlock their potential, and move from survival mode to **THRIVE MODE**. With compassion and a deep understanding of what students are going through, Philippa equips readers with the tools to thrive through university and beyond.

She lives in the UK with her husband and three children, and leads the growing **#ThriveModeMovement**, helping students, parents, and educators co-create a new wellbeing blueprint, one where health, happiness, and true success go hand in hand.

JOIN THE THRIVE MOVEMENT

You've just unlocked the tools to thrive. Now it's your turn to pass it on. Start Now. Pick just one THRIVE MODE hack and begin today.

Inspire: Others Share your wins, lessons, and lightbulb moments using #ThriveMode. You never know who needs to hear it.

Lead By Example: Host a Thrive Walk, study session, or breathwork break on your campus. Be the one who starts it. Others will follow.

Join the Community: Scan the QR code to join the Thrive Mode online space, a safe, supportive community for students who want to grow, share, and thrive together.

Stay in Touch With Me: I'd love to hear how you are getting on. Connect with me on all your favourite social media platforms @philippacharrier

Website: Subscribe to my newsletter for Thrive Mode tips, student hacks, and exclusive content. www.philippacharrier.com

Let's make thriving the new normal for university students. You're part of a movement rewriting the rules. You're in THRIVE MODE now. Welcome.

ENDNOTES